¡Sabroso!

NEW AMERICAN FAMILY COOKBOOKS
Capital's cooking series that focuses on treasured Old Country family recipes and how they are changed by new blended American families in our increasingly diverse culture.

OTHER TITLES IN THE SERIES INCLUDE:

Mangia Bene! The Italian American Family Cookbook
by Kate DeVivo

ALSO BY NOEMI CRISTINA TAYLOR

What Goes With What: Home Decorating Made Easy
co-authored by Lauren Smith

¡Sabroso!

The Spanish American Family Cookbook

NOEMI CRISTINA TAYLOR

Contributors:

NORA BRENNAN
NOHEMI BÁEZ HUMPHREY
ANA MARÍA HUTSON
LILLY NAUGHTON-CYPHERT

CAPITAL BOOKS, INC.
STERLING, VIRGINIA

Capital Books, Inc.
P.O. Box 605
Herndon, Virginia 20172-0605

Design and composition by Melissa Ehn and Sarah Lowe
at Wilsted & Taylor Publishing Services

Photos on pages 3, 168, and 198 by Judy Karpinski.
Photos on pages v, xii, 20, 26, 63, 122, 132, 214, 226, and 262 by Noemi C. Taylor.
Photo on page 250 by Fernando Baéz.

LIBRARY OF CONGRESS CATALOGING-IN-PUBLICATION DATA

Taylor, Noemi C.
    Sabroso! : a Spanish American family cookbook / Noemi Cristina
Taylor ; contributors Nora Brennan ... [et al.].—1st ed.
        p. cm. — (New American family cookbooks)
    Includes index.
    ISBN 1-892123-97-5 (alk. paper)
    1. Cookery, Spanish.   2. Cookery, American.   I. Brennan, Nora.
II. Title.   III. Series.
TX723.5.S7 T38   2002
641.59'268—dc21   2002067495

Printed in the United States of America on acid-free paper that
meets the American National Standards Institute Z39-48 Standard.

First Edition

10 9 8 7 6 5 4 3 2 1

To Mamá,
who taught me everything I know
about cooking and my heritage.
To Maddison and Finley,
who never turned down
a sample from the kitchen.

Nohemi (left)
with Noemi (right)

CONTENTS

ACKNOWLEDGMENTS

*T*hank you first and foremost to Nora, Nohemi, Ana, and Lilly for opening your hearts and your kitchens to me and patiently answering my every call for recipes and memories. Thank you to Kathleen Hughes for giving this labor of love a chance. Thank you to Judy Karpinski for providing editorial vision and advice along the way. Thank you to Emily Costello for excellent attention to detail.

INTRODUCTION

*S*abroso, which in Spanish means "tasty" and is exclaimed to compliment the chef, was initially inspired by my attempt to reproduce my mother's delicious recipe for *paella*, a traditional, savory Spanish rice dish. Over the telephone, she gave me the list of ingredients and patiently explained how to make the recipe to perfection. I had to search my local supermarkets for a few weeks before I was able to find one of the main ingredients in *paella*, a spice known as saffron, which lends the *paella* its rich flavor and yellow coloring. My search for saffron led me to wonder how mama had managed to make Spanish recipes, all the while living in a small town in the United States. She admitted that over the years she had adapted and adjusted the recipes to fit the ingredients she could find and the preferences of her American family. The recipes have become her version of the traditional recipes she grew up eating in her native country, Spain.

My mother, Nohemi, and her three best friends, Ana, Nora, and Lilly, came to the United States following love to start families of their own decades ago. In doing so, they left behind their native cultures and foods. When they settled in eastern Ohio, where not much cultural diversity exists, they found their way to each other through mutual friends and formed a friendship as close as any blood family—a cultural family linked by a common language and heritage.

Food has always been central to their friendship. As they discovered that American food and ingredients were different than those commonly used in their homelands, they began to adapt and change the foods they knew so well from their native countries. With every party, picnic, get-together, holiday, and celebration, they assigned dishes for each of them to contribute. The delicious foods available at these gatherings always reflected the eclectic variety of their four countries—Spain, Peru, Colombia, and Argentina. These recipes were swapped, discussed, and tweaked to suit their individual families and tastes. While the four ladies had many things in common—language, shared cultural characteristics, a basis in Spanish food—each of their countries has distinct culinary traditions. What emerged was a collection of recipes whose roots resided in their native homelands, but which have been augmented and adapted to fit American ingredients and tastes. You can find almost all the ingredients in the recipes in any grocery store, although you may have to search a little harder for some specialty ingredients. Whenever possible use the freshest ingredients you can obtain.

Although a native of Madrid, Spain, I grew up in the United States, far away from my cultural heritage. I have been fortunate to be surrounded by these vibrant and creative women who wrapped their families in the traditions and foods that would always remind us of where we came from. Throughout the years, I have enjoyed many of these recipes. Now I hope that you will enjoy them also.

From left to right:
Nora, Nohemi,
Ana, and Lilly

¡Sabroso!

Appetizers

- TAPAS 2
- SQUID WITH RED WINE SAUCE 4
  Calamares con Salsa de Vino • *Spain*
- MARINATED SEA BASS 5
  Ceviche de Corvina • *Colombia*
- SPANISH OMELET 6
  Tortilla • *Spain*
- CHIPS WITH AVOCADO DIP 7
  Salsa de Aguacate • *Colombia*
- ASPARAGUS WITH TOMATO VINAIGRETTE 8
  Espárragos Vinagreta • *Spain*
- ASPARAGUS VINAIGRETTE 9
  Espárragos a la Vinagreta • *Argentina*
- GREEN PLANTAIN CHIPS 10
  Patacones • *Colombia*
- SEVILLIAN EGGS 11
  Huevos Sevillanos • *Spain*
- MARINATED MANGO 12
  Ceviche de Mango • *Colombia*
- HONEYDEW MELON WITH PROSCIUTTO 13
  Melón con Jamón • *Argentina*
- CREAM CHEESE BALL 14
  Bollos de Cuajada • *Colombia*

*T*apas are small portions of foods, served both hot and cold. While typically in Spanish bars *tapas* are part of a drink order, many of these delicious foods also make wonderful appetizers to start any meal and are even served as meals by themselves. There are many different *tapas* foods, including cheeses and hams, omelets *(tortillas)* and sausages, olives and anchovies, clams, sardines, mussels, and tuna. *Tapas* are often served with bread that is dribbled with olive oil and garlic. Originally, this mouthful of food was designed to accompany the order of a drink. While their origins are unknown, the most widely held belief is that they came to be called *tapas*, which means covers, when they were served on small plates on top of a glass of sherry to prevent flies from entering the glass. In Spain, the *tapas* bar is the center of social life in small villages and large cities. *Tapa* hopping is a way of life there, where friends stop by various bars and have several glasses of wine to sample the *tapa* specialties in each. *Tapas* bars have recently become popular in many areas of the United States. In restaurants, almost every Spanish food comes in the form of *tapas* and they're a good way to sample the rich variety of Spanish cuisine.   —Noemi

In León, the northern city where I was born, there is a neighborhood called *El Barrio Húmedo,* which is the center of social life for the city. There are about eighteen to twenty small bars in the neighborhood as well as churches, shops, homes, and some government buildings. *El Barrio Húmedo* is located in the oldest part of the city and has a pedestrian walkway where people, young or old, friends or family, couples or groups, stroll through catching up and stopping in at the bars for a glass of wine, beer, or juice and of course the large variety of *tapas* offered.   —Nohemi

What the Spaniards call *tapas,* the Argentineans call *platitos* (small dishes). In Buenos Aires, the capital city of Argentina, people gather with their friends before dinner, usually around seven o'clock in the evening. They order *aperitivo con platitos* (a drink with appetizers), something like gin and tonic, a martini on the rocks, a beer, or a glass of wine. The server brings out at least ten *platitos* in the first round that can include peanuts, cheeses, prosciutto, olives, seafood, and salami. When you are done, another round of *platitos* is brought out. All this food is a compelling reason why dinner in Argentina starts around nine or ten o'clock.   —Lilly

An assortment of tapas

Squid with Red Wine Sauce

Calamares con Salsa de Vino ◆ *Spain*

I love cooking with wine, not just a glass in my hand, but splashing a bit into various recipes. Wine really adds to the flavor of many foods.
—Nohemi

½ cup olive oil

4 tablespoons chopped fresh
   parsley

6 garlic cloves, minced

1 pound squid, cleaned

2 red bell peppers, chopped

1 large onion, chopped

1 large tomato, chopped

½ cup dry red wine

Salt and pepper

For the marinade, mix together ¼ cup of the oil, 2 tablespoons of the parsley, and half of the minced garlic in a small bowl. Cut the squid into even rings and place in a bowl, reserving the tentacles. Pour the marinade over the squid and let marinate in refrigerator for 2 hours. Heat the remaining ¼ cup oil in a large skillet over medium heat. Add vegetables, the other half of the garlic, and squid tentacles. Simmer until vegetables are tender, about 15 minutes. Stir in the wine and simmer an additional 5 minutes. Season with salt and pepper and add the remaining 2 tablespoons parsley. Add squid rings and fry 2 minutes longer or until squid is opaque.

◆ *4 to 6 servings*

Marinated Sea Bass

CEVICHE DE CORVINA ◆ *Colombia*

This dish may be served with crackers on the side.   —Nora

1 pound sea bass fillet, cut into
    small pieces
3 tablespoons finely chopped onion
1 tablespoon chopped celery
2 tablespoons chopped fresh
    coriander

2 cups fresh lemon juice
½ teaspoon Worcestershire sauce
Salt and pepper
Tabasco sauce
Ketchup

Combine all ingredients in a glass bowl, adding salt, pepper, and Tabasco sauce to taste. Let stand for at least 4 hours in the refrigerator. Spoon into small bowls and top with ketchup.

◆ *4 to 6 servings*

Spanish Omelet

TORTILLA ◆ *Spain*

This traditional Spanish dish can be served cold as an appetizer or hot as a side dish. Usually it is made just from potatoes but you can also add green or red bell peppers to spice it up a bit. Accompanied by a salad and dessert (which in my house is usually fresh fruit) this recipe also makes a complete meal.   —Nohemi

One of my favorite foods growing up, I have successfully adapted this recipe and added it to my repertoire. I admit, it was a little tricky to learn how to flip the *tortilla* and pan over on a plate without spilling anything, but practice makes perfect and my *tortillas* come out round and thick. I like to serve it as a hot side to meat or chicken.   —Noemi

Olive oil

1 pound potatoes, peeled and
    thinly sliced

1 medium onion, thinly sliced

Salt

4 eggs

1 tablespoon olive oil

Over medium heat add enough oil to cover bottom of a skillet. Layer potatoes and onion. Cover and cook until tender. Season with salt to taste and set aside. Beat eggs in a bowl. Add the potato mixture to the eggs and mix well. Heat a skillet over medium low heat with 1 tablespoon oil. Pour mixture into skillet. Cook until bottom is just golden and top still uncooked, about 5 minutes. Loosen sides with a spatula and slide onto a large plate. Cover the plate with the skillet and invert the plate. Return the omelet, cooked side up, to skillet, return to stove and cook 3 more minutes. Cut omelet into wedges and serve.

◆ *4 to 6 servings*

Chips with Avocado Dip

Salsa de Aguacate ◆ *Colombia*

I n Colombia, this appetizer is served with drinks on a hot day, along with hot tortillas or tortilla chips.   —Nora

2 ripe avocados, pitted, peeled, and finely chopped

1 small tomato, skinned and chopped

Juice of 1 lemon

2 tablespoons chopped onion

½ teaspoon chopped jalapeño pepper

Tabasco sauce

Salt and pepper

Combine avocados, tomato, lemon juice, and onion in a blender or food processor. Process until mixture is lumpy. Add Tabasco sauce and salt and pepper to taste.

◆ *4 to 6 servings*

Asparagus with Tomato Vinaigrette

Espárragos Vinagreta ◆ *Spain*

1 pound asparagus, ends trimmed	2 green onions, chopped
¼ cup olive oil	1 tablespoon chopped fresh parsley
¼ cup red wine vinegar	Salt and pepper
1 small tomato, chopped	1 hard-boiled egg, chopped
¼ red bell pepper, chopped	

Cook the asparagus in boiling water until tender, about 5 minutes. Drain, then run under cold water and drain again. Arrange asparagus on a large platter and refrigerate, covered, until cold. To make the vinaigrette, mix the oil and vinegar. Add the tomato, red pepper, green onions, and parsley. Season with salt and pepper to taste. Pour half of the vinaigrette over the asparagus. Garnish with the hard-boiled egg. Serve and offer the remaining dressing separately.

◆ *4 to 6 servings*

◆

Summer Picnic

APPETIZER ◆ SPAIN

Asparagus with Tomato
Vinaigrette 8
Espárragos Vinagreta

SIDE ◆ COLOMBIA

Lemon Green Beans 61
Chauchas con Limón

MAIN ◆ ARGENTINA

Chimichurri Steak 158
Carne Chimichurri

DESSERT ◆ PERU

Mango Cream 249
Crema de Mango

◆ ◆ ◆

Asparagus Vinaigrette

Espárragos a la Vinagreta ◆ *Argentina*

I choose asparagus that are young and tender.
They are the best kind for this recipe.   —Lilly

2 pounds medium asparagus
  spears
¼ cup cider vinegar
1 tablespoon chopped fresh parsley
2 hard-boiled eggs (yolks only),
  chopped

1 teaspoon mustard
Salt and pepper
½ cup olive oil

Wash the asparagus thoroughly and trim about 1 inch off the bottom. Cook
in boiling, salted water until they are tender. Drain and arrange on a salad
plate. In a medium bowl, blend vinegar, parsley, egg yolks, and mustard.
Add salt and pepper to taste and then add the oil. Mix well. Pour vinaigrette on top of the asparagus. Refrigerate for at least 1 hour so the flavors
can blend.

◆ *4 to 6 servings*

Green Plantain Chips

Patacones ◆ *Colombia*

Fried plantain slices are very popular in many parts of South America. They are often sprinkled with salt and served with drinks as appetizers. You can also substitute the plantains with green bananas.   —Nora

Vegetable oil
1 large plantain, peeled and sliced in 1½-inch slices

Pour oil into a pan or fryer to a depth of 2 to 3 inches. Heat to 325°F. Drop in the plantain slices and fry until they are tender, about 5 minutes. Lift out and drain on paper towels. Cover each slice with wax paper and mash it hard with a wooden mallet. Raise the temperature to 375°F and fry the slices until they are brown and crispy outside and tender inside.

◆ *4 to 6 servings*

Sevillian Eggs

Huevos Sevillanos ◆ *Spain*

½ cup olive oil

1 onion, chopped

1 garlic clove, minced

1 cup chopped green bell pepper

½ cup red pimientos

2 large tomatoes, chopped

Pinch of oregano

Dash of Tabasco sauce

Salt and pepper

6 eggs

¼ cup shredded Swiss cheese

¼ cup black olives, chopped

Heat ¼ cup of the oil in a skillet. Add onion, garlic, bell pepper, and pimentos. Sauté until tender. Add tomatoes. Cook until the mixture thickens. Stir in the oregano and Tabasco sauce and add salt and pepper to taste. Heat the remaining ¼ cup oil in a skillet. Crack the eggs into the skillet one at a time. Fry until the whites are set. Sprinkle with Swiss cheese. Cover and fry 2 more minutes. Arrange the eggs on a serving dish, top with the vegetables, and garnish with chopped black olives.

◆ 4 to 6 servings

Marinated Mango

Ceviche de Mango ◆ *Colombia*

This dish may be served with crackers.   —Nora

10 very green mangos, pitted,
    peeled, and finely diced
2 tablespoons ketchup
½ teaspoon mustard

2 tablespoons finely chopped onion
1 teaspoon salt
2 teaspoons Worcestershire sauce

Combine all ingredients in a bowl and refrigerate before serving.

◆ *4 to 6 servings*

Honeydew Melon with Prosciutto

Melón con Jamón ◆ *Argentina*

Festive toothpicks can be used to pierce the melon pieces.   —Lilly

1 medium ripe honeydew melon or cantaloupe, cut into 3-inch pieces
½ pound prosciutto, thinly sliced

Wrap prosciutto slices around each piece of melon and arrange on a nice dish.

◆ *4 to 6 servings*

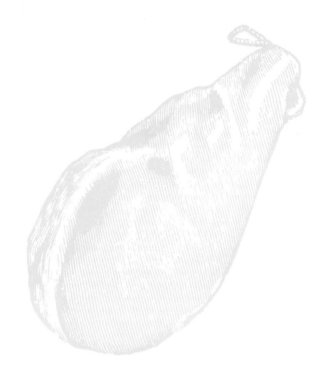

Cream Cheese Ball

Bollos de Cuajada ◆ *Colombia*

Olive oil

½ cup flour

9 eggs

1 teaspoon grated lemon zest

4 packages (32 ounces) cream
cheese

Grated nutmeg

In a large bowl, mix flour, eggs, lemon zest, and cream cheese. Roll into
1½-inch balls and fry them until crispy in a pan with 2 to 3 inches of oil.
Remove and drain on a paper towel. Roll in nutmeg and serve.

◆ *4 to 6 servings*

Soups

- CREAM OF COCONUT SOUP 30
  Sopa de Crema de Coco • *Colombia*

- CREAM OF SQUASH SOUP 31
  Crema de Zapallo • *Peru*

- WINTER SQUASH SOUP 32
  Sopa de Zapallo • *Colombia*

- NORA'S POTATO SOUP 33
  Sopa de Locro • *Colombia*

- ANA'S POTATO SOUP 34
  Sopa Crema de Papas • *Peru*

- SWEET POTATO SOUP 35
  Sopa de Camote • *Colombia*

- GARLIC SOUP 36
  Sopa de Ajo • *Peru*

- PLANTAIN SOUP 37
  Sopa de Banana Verde • *Colombia*

- ZUCCHINI PUREE 38
  Puré de Calabacín • *Spain*

- CABBAGE SOUP 39
  Sopa de Repollo • *Colombia*

- PEASANT SOUP 40
  Sopa Paisana • *Peru*

Peruvian Vegetable Soup

Sopa de Gazpacho ✦ *Peru*

Soup is very popular in Latin America. Most countries regard it as a main dish. *Gazpacho* is one such soup served in several Spanish-speaking countries. Here is Ana's adaptation of a recipe from Peru that leaves the vegetables lumpy. Nohemi's recipe that follows, from Spain, purees the vegetables to make a smoother consistency. *Gazpacho* is usually served cold. I remember having this delicious treat on hot summer days. Serve this soup with garlic bread.   —Noemi

5 tomatoes, peeled, seeded, and finely chopped

1 cucumber, peeled, seeded, and chopped

1 cup finely chopped onion

1 green bell pepper, seeded and chopped

Salt and pepper

1 teaspoon garlic juice

¼ cup olive oil

¼ cup fresh lemon juice

Dash of cayenne

2 cups tomato juice

In a bowl, combine tomatoes, cucumber, onion, and green bell pepper. Mix well. Season with salt and pepper to taste. Let set at room temperature 2 hours for flavors to blend. Add remaining ingredients and mix well. Chill thoroughly before serving.

✦ *4 to 6 servings*

Spanish Vegetable Soup

Gazpacho ✦ *Spain*

Typical of Andalucia, a region in southern Spain, this is a colorful summer soup. Once served, you can add diced tomatoes, green bell peppers, and cucumbers to your bowl if you wish.   —Nohemi

1½ pounds ripe tomatoes, peeled
   and seeded
1 cup cubed French bread
1 small cucumber, peeled
½ medium onion
1 small green bell pepper, seeded

1 cup olive oil
1 garlic clove, peeled
2 tablespoons vinegar
Salt and pepper

Put all the ingredients except the salt and pepper in a blender or food processor, and puree them in batches, adding a little water if necessary. Season with salt and pepper to taste and refrigerate 8 to 12 hours or until chilled thoroughly.

✦ *4 to 6 servings*

NORA

Colombia's geographical and cultural variety lends itself to a vast repertoire of foods. Native Indian and Spanish influences impacted the evolution of the Colombian cooking style. Shellfish is very common in the Pacific Coast and Bogota, the capital, is known widely for its perfect soups and rice dishes. When she relocated to America twenty-four years ago, Nora learned how to incorporate these foods into American meals to please her husband, Don, and son, Samuel. The Colombians eat all kinds of meat but Nora grew up eating more fish and she was amazed to see Americans consuming so much red meat. Nora's recipes reflect her taste in soups, rice, and shellfish.   —Noemi

I didn't understand how revealing it would be to go searching through the recipes that I contributed to this book. I was surprised at how a recipe could tie together a family sharing. I am glad I have a lot of sisters that along with my mamá (she raised a family of nine, five daughters and four sons) taught me how to share many things—among them, recipes—through our years of growing up. Christmas, the

New Year, Easter, birthdays, *desayuno* (breakfast), *almuerzo* (lunch), *merienda* (snack), and *comida* (dinner) were full of love and cooking and I am thankful for that. I tried to incorporate that sense of food and love in my everyday life with my husband and son and my family and friends and let them experience the joy of Colombian cuisine. Today I am a hair designer and life has changed but I still enjoy cooking when I have the time.   —Nora

Nora (center) with Nohemi (left) and Ana (right)

Tomato Soup

SOPA DE TOMATES ◆ *Colombia*

I am especially fond of soups. A soup can help to balance a simple dish, can be a main course that, with easy ingredients such as vegetables, beans, poultry, shellfish, wine, cream, or cuts of meat, can satisfy anyone. This is a very fresh and simple tomato soup best made when tomatoes reach their peak season and are ripe and sweet. It can be served with French bread.
   —Nora

2 tablespoons butter

1 large onion, finely chopped

1 garlic clove, chopped

6 large tomatoes, peeled and
   coarsely chopped

4 cups chicken stock (preferably
   homemade)

Salt and pepper

¼ cup dry sherry

1 tablespoon chopped fresh parsley

Melt the butter in a fairly large saucepan and sauté the onion and garlic until onion is soft. Add tomatoes and cook, stirring, for 3 minutes. Pour in stock and simmer for another 10 minutes. Cool slightly and puree in several batches in blender or food processor. Reheat, adding salt and pepper to taste and the sherry. Garnish with parsley.

◆ *4 to 6 servings*

Lentil Soup

Potaje de Lentejas ◆ *Peru*

T his soup may be served with corn bread.   —Ana

2 cups lentils

2 tablespoons olive oil

5 strips smoked bacon, cut into
  small strips

1 medium onion, chopped

½ cup chopped celery

2 carrots, cubed

1 bay leaf

½ jalapeño or chili pepper, seeded
  and chopped

1 green bell pepper, seeded and
  chopped

2 potatoes, peeled and cubed

6 cups chicken stock

½ cup chopped Canadian bacon

Salt and pepper

Wash lentils twice and drain. In a medium saucepan, bring 2 quarts of
water to a boil. Add the lentils and boil for 5 minutes. Drain and reserve.
In a heavy skillet, heat the olive oil. Add the smoked bacon and cook until
they are crispy. Remove to a platter. Add the onion, celery, carrots, bay leaf,
jalapeño, green bell pepper, and potatoes to the bacon drippings. Mix well.
Cook until vegetables are al dente. Add the chicken stock, Canadian bacon,
and smoked bacon strips. Stir. Add the lentils. Reduce heat to low and cook
for about 15 minutes or until soup is thick and vegetables are tender. Add
salt and pepper to taste.

◆ *4 to 6 servings*

Chickpea Soup

Sopa de Garbanzos ◆ *Colombia*

This soup may be served with corn bread or French bread.   —Nora

2 tablespoons vegetable oil
1 medium onion, finely chopped
1 garlic clove, minced
1 green bell pepper, seeded and
    chopped
½ jalapeño pepper, seeded and
    chopped

4 cups beef or chicken stock
1 cup chickpeas, soaked for 4 hours
    or overnight
Salt and pepper
1 tablespoon chopped fresh parsley

Drain the chickpeas, cover them with fresh water, and boil for 10 minutes. Lower heat and simmer until soft, about 1 hour. Set aside. Heat the oil in a skillet and sauté onion and garlic until soft. Add bell pepper and jalapeño. Sauté for another minute. Transfer mixture to a blender or food processor. Add stock to the mixture and puree. Pour the mixture into a medium-sized pan. Put the cooked chickpeas with their liquid in a blender or food processor and puree. Add the chickpea puree to the onion mixture. Season to taste with salt and pepper. Cook, stirring from time to time, for about 30 minutes, until all the flavors are blended. Garnish with parsley.

◆ *4 to 6 servings*

Dry Cod Soup

PORRUSALDA ◆ *Spain*

Growing up, we were nine brothers and sisters, so the house was always full of lively children. Papá was self-employed and was able to spend a lot of time with us. I remember coming home for dinner from one of our adventures and Papá sat all of us on top of the table. Mamá gave him a big bowl of soup and a spoon. He took turns feeding each of us as we giggled and talked about the day's adventures.   —Nohemi

½ pound dry, salted cod

¼ cup olive oil

6 medium leeks, cut into
    bite-sized pieces

1 ½ pounds potatoes, peeled
    and diced

Salt

The day before soup is to be served, soak dry cod in cold water, changing water several times to desalt. In a saucepan with 2 cups of water, bring cod to a boil. As soon as it starts boiling, take cod out and let it cool. Peel skin, take off bones, and crumble. Place cod back in the saucepan with the hot water. Reserve. Heat oil in another saucepan. Add leeks. Sauté 5 minutes and add potatoes. Sauté another 5 minutes. Add 2 quarts of water and cook for 35 minutes, or until potatoes are tender but not soft. Add cod and the water and cook for 10 minutes. Add salt if necessary.

◆ *4 servings*

Nohemi (center) surrounded by her family on a trip to Spain

Clam Soup

SOPA DE ALMEJAS ◆ *Colombia*

¼ cup olive oil

1 medium onion, finely chopped

1 garlic clove, chopped

1 green bell pepper, seeded
    and chopped

1 red bell pepper, seeded
    and chopped

3 medium tomatoes, seeded
    and chopped

1 pound potatoes, peeled and sliced

1 bay leaf

Pinch of ground cloves

Pinch of oregano

Salt and pepper

3 dozen clams, washed

2 pounds firm white fish, cut into
    pieces

2 cups clam juice

2 cups water

1 tablespoon chopped fresh parsley

Heat the oil in a flameproof casserole and sauté the onion, garlic, and peppers until the onion is soft. Add the tomatoes and sauté 2 minutes longer. Add the potatoes, bay leaf, ground cloves, and oregano. Season with salt and pepper to taste. Cover and simmer until potatoes are tender. Add clams, pieces of fish, clam juice, and water. Cover and simmer for another 10 minutes, or until the clams have opened and fish is done. Sprinkle with parsley before serving.

◆ *4 to 6 servings*

Mallorcan Soup

Sopa de Mallorca ◆ *Spain*

2 tablespoons olive oil

2 onions, chopped

2 garlic cloves, chopped

2 green bell peppers, seeded
   and chopped

3 tomatoes, peeled and chopped

3 tablespoons chopped fresh
   parsley

1 medium cabbage, shredded

2 quarts boiling water

Salt and pepper

Heat the oil in a saucepan and sauté the onions, garlic, and bell peppers until soft. Add tomatoes, parsley, and cabbage. Once the vegetables are tender, add a little less than 2 quarts of boiling water and simmer for 30 to 40 minutes. Add salt and pepper to taste before serving.

◆ *4 to 6 servings*

*Nohemi stirring a pot
of delicious soup*

Ana's Corn Soup

Sopa de Maiz ◆ *Peru*

4 cups fresh corn kernels
1 cup chicken stock
4 tablespoons butter
½ cup chopped green onions
3½ cups milk
Salt

3 tablespoons chopped green
   chilies
6 tablespoons sour cream
Tortilla chips
1 tablespoon chopped fresh
   cilantro

Combine corn kernels and chicken stock in a blender or food processor. Puree to a smooth consistency. Melt butter in a large saucepan. Wilt the green onions in butter. Add corn puree. Simmer for 5 minutes or until thickened. Add milk, and salt to taste. Cook 15 minutes at low heat. Divide the chopped chilies among 6 soup bowls. Pour soup into bowls. Garnish each with a tablespoon of sour cream, a few tortilla chips, and cilantro before serving.

◆ *4 to 6 servings*

Nora's Corn Soup

Sopa de Elote ◆ *Colombia*

4 cups fresh corn kernels, or if
    frozen, thawed
2 cups chicken stock
1 cup light cream

Salt and pepper
2 eggs, beaten
2 tablespoons chopped fresh
    parsley

Put the corn into a blender or food processor with the chicken stock and blend to puree. Pour the puree into a saucepan, stir in cream, and simmer at low heat, stirring from time to time. Cook for about 5 minutes. Work the mixture through a sieve, return it to the saucepan and season with salt and pepper to taste. If too thick, add a little more stock or cream. Bring to a simmer. Stir ½ cup of the soup into the beaten eggs, mix well, then stir the egg mixture into the soup and cook 1 or 2 more minutes. Serve garnished with the parsley.

◆ 4 to 6 servings

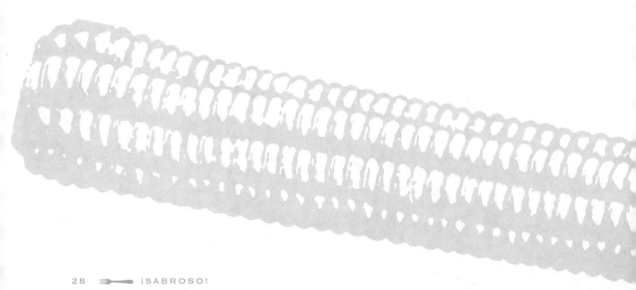

Cream of Celery Soup

CREMA DE APIO ◆ *Spain*

Abouquet garni is an herb mixture that is tied together and flavors a dish. —Noemi

4 tablespoons olive oil

2 celery stalks, cut into large
  pieces

2 large onions, cut into large pieces

2 quarts boiling water

1 soup bone

Bouquet garni of 1 garlic clove and
  1 bay leaf

Salt and pepper

2 tablespoons butter

$\frac{1}{4}$ cup flour

2 cups milk

2 egg yolks

$\frac{1}{2}$ cup heavy cream

1 tablespoon chopped fresh parsley

1 tablespoon chopped celery leaves

In a large saucepan, heat 2 tablespoons of the oil. Add celery and onions. Sauté for about 2 minutes and add boiling water and the soup bone. Add bouquet garni, and salt and pepper to taste. Simmer for 1 $\frac{1}{2}$ hours. Remove the soup bone and bouquet garni. In small batches, puree in a blender or food processor and set aside. In a large saucepan, heat butter and the remaining 2 tablespoons of oil. Stir in flour and add milk, stirring constantly. Cook for 5 minutes. Add puree and simmer for 10 minutes. In a serving bowl, beat 2 egg yolks and the heavy cream. A little at a time, add soup so as not to scramble the egg. Before serving, sprinkle with parsley and chopped leaves of celery.

◆ *4 to 6 servings*

Cream of Coconut Soup

Sopa de Crema de Coco • *Colombia*

This is a classic soup from the region of Cartagena, a coastal city of Colombia.   —Nora

1 medium coconut	1 medium onion, grated
5 cups chicken stock	2 tablespoons flour
2 tablespoons butter	Salt and pepper

With an ice pick, screwdriver, or similar sharp implement, pierce 2 or 3 holes in the coconut, using a hammer to bang it. Drain the coconut milk and reserve. Tap the coconut all over with the hammer to break the nut into pieces. Shred the white meat and place in a bowl. Heat 1 cup of the chicken stock and pour over the shredded coconut and let stand for 30 minutes. Strain it. This will make a thin coconut milk. Heat the butter in a saucepan and sauté the onion until soft. Stir in the flour and cook, stirring, over low heat for 3 minutes. Gradually whisk in the thin coconut milk, the reserved coconut milk, and then the rest of the stock. Season with salt and pepper to taste.

◆ *4 to 6 servings*

Cream of Squash Soup

CREMA DE ZAPALLO ◆ *Peru*

This soup may be garnished with croutons, freshly chopped parsley, and grated Parmesan cheese.   —Ana

1 pound yellow squash, peeled
   and cubed
¼ pound potatoes, peeled
   and cubed
¼ pound carrots, chopped

1 teaspoon chopped onion
1 cube chicken bouillon
Pinch of garlic salt
Salt and pepper
1 tablespoon butter

Combine all the ingredients, except the butter, in a small saucepan with 2 cups of water and boil until tender. Using a blender or food processor, puree the ingredients until the mixture is creamy. Return to the saucepan and let simmer at low heat for 3 to 5 minutes. Stir in butter before serving.

◆ *4 to 6 servings*

◆

Autumn Harvest

SOUP ◆ PERU

Cream of Squash Soup 31
Crema de Zapallo

SIDE ◆ COLOMBIA

Colombian Turnovers 69
Empanadas a la Santa Fe

MAIN ◆ SPAIN

Orange Pork Loin 135
Lomo a la Naranja

DESSERT ◆ ARGENTINA

Banana and Pineapple Cake 241
Torta de Banana y Anana

◆ ◆ ◆

Winter Squash Soup

Sopa de Zapallo ◆ *Colombia*

This soup may be topped with grated Parmesan cheese and served with pita bread.   —Nora

4 tablespoons butter

3 green onions, chopped

1 jalapeño pepper, seeded
   and chopped

2 garlic cloves, minced

2 pounds winter squash, seeded,
   peeled and cut into small pieces

4 cups chicken stock

Salt and pepper

1 teaspoon honey

½ cup light cream

2 tablespoons chopped
   fresh parsley

Melt the butter in a saucepan. Add the onions, jalapeño, and garlic. Cook until the mixture is soft. Mix well. Add the squash and the stock to the saucepan. Add salt and pepper to taste, and the honey. Simmer for 20 minutes or until the squash is tender and the mixture is thick. Add the cream and sprinkle with parsley.

◆ *4 to 6 servings*

Nora's Potato Soup

Sopa de Locro ◆ *Colombia*

1 tablespoon butter

1 medium onion, chopped

4 cups chicken stock

1 pound red potatoes, peeled
  and finely chopped

2 cups half-and-half

½ cup shredded Cheddar cheese

1 teaspoon paprika

Salt and pepper

In large pan, melt butter and stir in the onion. Sauté over medium heat until onion is soft. Add chicken stock. Bring to boil, add potatoes and simmer over low heat, uncovered, stirring occasionally. When the potatoes are done, add the half-and-half. Continue to cook, stirring from time to time, until the potatoes start to disintegrate. Stir the Cheddar cheese into the soup. Season with paprika, and salt and pepper to taste.

◆ *4 to 6 servings*

Ana's Potato Soup

SOPA CREMA DE PAPAS ◆ *Peru*

3 tablespoons butter	1 quart hot milk
3 green onions, chopped	Salt and pepper
½ cup chopped ham	Paprika
4 large potatoes, peeled and sliced	½ cup shredded Cheddar cheese

Melt the butter, stir in the onions, and sauté over medium heat. Add the ham and mix well. Add potatoes. Add ¾ cup of water and cover. Cook until both potatoes and onions are soft enough to put through a sieve. After the mixture has been sieved, add hot milk to it, stirring constantly. Season with salt, pepper, and paprika to taste. Stir in the Cheddar cheese before serving.

◆ *4 to 6 servings*

Sweet Potato Soup

SOPA DE CAMOTE ◆ *Colombia*

I use both yams and sweet potatoes for this recipe. You can choose either depending on your taste.   —Nora

1 pound yams or sweet potatoes	2 cups chicken stock
4 tablespoons butter	2 cups half-and-half
1 medium onion, chopped	Salt and pepper
4 medium tomatoes, peeled and chopped	1 tablespoon chopped fresh parsley
	1 teaspoon chopped fresh basil

Peel and cut potatoes in chunks and boil until tender. Drain and chop the chunks coarsely. Melt butter, stir in the onion, and sauté. Add tomatoes and cook for about 5 minutes. Put mixture into blender or food processor with potatoes, chicken stock, and half-and-half. Reduce to a smooth puree and return to pan. Simmer for 10 minutes and add salt and pepper to taste. Garnish with parsley and basil before serving.

◆ *4 to 6 servings*

Garlic Soup

Sopa de Ajo ◆ *Peru*

⅓ cup olive oil

4 tablespoons butter

8 garlic cloves, peeled

½ teaspoon paprika

Dash of cayenne

Salt and pepper

3 cups bread cubes

6 cups chicken stock

Heat oil and butter in a skillet. Add garlic and sauté until golden brown. Remove garlic, mash, and reserve. Stir in paprika, cayenne, and salt and pepper to taste. Add bread cubes. Fry until golden brown. Remove and reserve. Add chicken stock to oil. Using a little water, form a paste with the reserved garlic. Add garlic paste to the soup and bring to a boil. Reduce heat and simmer for 30 minutes. Ladle soup into serving bowls. Serve with the fried bread cubes.

◆ *4 to 6 servings*

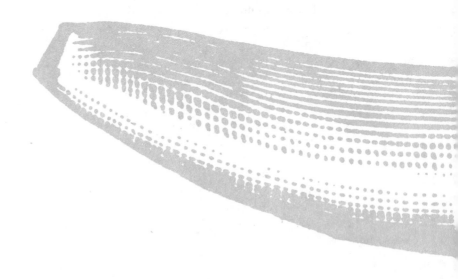

Plantain Soup

Sopa de Banana Verde • *Colombia*

Traditionally, plantains for this soup are grated. I use a food processor, which does the job just as effectively.   —Nora

1 green plantain
6 cups chicken stock (preferably homemade)
Salt and pepper

Grate the plantain or blend in a food processor with a little of the chicken stock. Pour the remaining chicken stock in a saucepan and heat. Add the plantain and cook over moderate heat, stirring from time to time until the mixture is thick. Season with salt and pepper to taste. Simmer uncovered for another 10 minutes before serving.

◆ *4 to 6 servings*

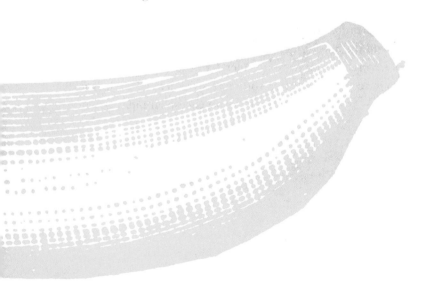

Zucchini Puree

Puŕe de Calabacín ◆ *Spain*

My youngest sister, María, who lives in Madrid, makes a delicious zucchini puree. She serves it cold in the summer. I don't know how she makes it so tasty, but when I make this recipe I always think of her. Chopped hard-boiled eggs may replace the Parmesan cheese garnish.
—Nohemi

3 tablespoons olive oil

1 onion, chopped

3 carrots, chopped

1 tablespoon chopped fresh parsley

3 zucchinis, chopped

4 cups chicken, beef, or
   vegetable stock

2 eggs

Salt and pepper

2 tablespoons fresh grated
   Parmesan cheese

In a saucepan, sauté the onion in oil. Add the carrots and the parsley. Once vegetables are soft, add the zucchini and when it is done add the stock. Let it boil and then cool. Puree the mixture in a blender or food processor. Beat the eggs and add to puree little by little. Add more stock if needed. Season with salt and pepper to taste. Serve with Parmesan cheese on top.

◆ *4 to 6 servings*

Cabbage Soup

Sopa de Repollo ◆ *Colombia*

Colombia's sunny climate produces lovely fruits and vegetables and the cabbages are no exception. I choose a firm green cabbage, which is the best kind for this soup. This may be served with French bread.   —Nora

2 tablespoons butter

1 small cabbage (about 1 pound), finely shredded

2 medium potatoes, peeled and cut into thin slices

2 green onions, chopped

1 green bell pepper, seeded and chopped

1 red bell pepper, seeded and chopped

½ jalapeño or chili pepper, seeded and finely chopped

4 cups of chicken stock (preferably homemade)

Salt and pepper

1 cup shredded Cheddar cheese

Melt butter in a skillet or saucepan. Add cabbage, potatoes, onions, and all peppers and stir to blend. Cook until all the vegetables are tender, about 2 to 3 minutes. Pour in stock. Season with salt and pepper to taste. Simmer at low heat for about 30 minutes or until the cabbage is cooked. Stir in the Cheddar cheese before serving.

◆ *4 to 6 servings*

Peasant Soup

SOPA PAISANA ◆ *Peru*

This soup may be served with corn bread.   —Ana

1 cup dried beans, such as red
    kidney beans

2 tablespoons olive oil

1 bay leaf

1 onion, chopped

½ cup chopped celery

3 carrots, cubed

1 medium turnip, cubed

2 garlic cloves, minced

½ pound smoked ham, cubed

¼ pound lean salt pork

Salt and pepper

½ cup cooked rice

In a medium saucepan, bring the beans and 2 quarts of water to a boil over high heat and boil for 2 minutes. Remove from heat and let beans soak for 1 hour. Drain beans, saving water. In a heavy skillet, heat the olive oil. Add the bay leaf, onion, celery, carrots, turnip, and garlic. Sauté for a few minutes. Add the ham, reserved water from the beans, salt pork, and cooked beans. Mix well. Season with salt and pepper to taste. Bring to a boil, reduce heat, and simmer for 2 hours. Discard the salt pork and skim the fat off the soup. With a slotted spoon, remove about half the bean mixture and puree in a blender or food processor. Return to soup. Simmer over low heat for another 10 minutes. Add the cooked rice and stir well before serving.

◆ *4 to 6 servings*

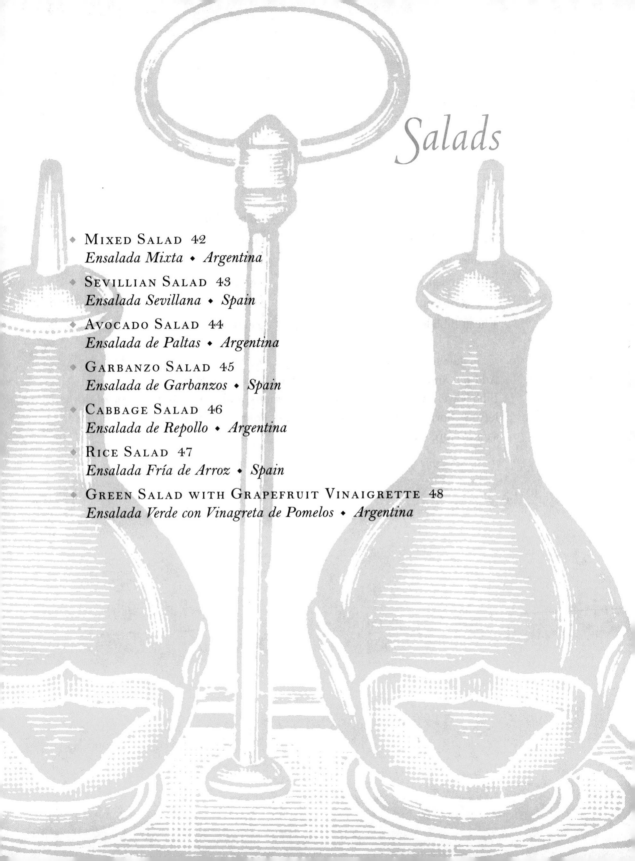

Salads

- MIXED SALAD 42
  Ensalada Mixta ◆ *Argentina*

- SEVILLIAN SALAD 43
  Ensalada Sevillana ◆ *Spain*

- AVOCADO SALAD 44
  Ensalada de Paltas ◆ *Argentina*

- GARBANZO SALAD 45
  Ensalada de Garbanzos ◆ *Spain*

- CABBAGE SALAD 46
  Ensalada de Repollo ◆ *Argentina*

- RICE SALAD 47
  Ensalada Fría de Arroz ◆ *Spain*

- GREEN SALAD WITH GRAPEFRUIT VINAIGRETTE 48
  Ensalada Verde con Vinagreta de Pomelos ◆ *Argentina*

Mixed Salad

Ensalada Mixta ◆ *Argentina*

6 tablespoons olive oil

2 tablespoons sherry vinegar

1 tablespoon fresh lemon juice

Salt and pepper

1 head Boston lettuce

1 head Bibb lettuce

4 large ripe tomatoes, sliced

1 can (6 ounces) tuna fish,
   drained and flaked

2 green onions, chopped

2 tablespoons whole green olives

½ cup crumbled feta cheese

To make vinaigrette, whisk oil, vinegar, and lemon juice in a small bowl. Add salt and pepper to taste and mix well. Line a platter with Boston and Bibb leaves. Arrange tomatoes, tuna, onions, and green olives on top of the lettuce. Sprinkle the feta cheese over all. Pour the vinaigrette on top of the salad before serving.

◆ *4 to 6 servings*

Sevillian Salad

Ensalada Sevillana   ◆   *Spain*

Salad

½ cup cooked rice

3 red bell peppers, seeded
    and cut into strips

6 green onions, chopped

4 tomatoes, sliced

7 ounces whole green
    or black olives

Vinaigrette

1 garlic clove, minced

2 tablespoons sherry vinegar

2 tablespoons olive oil

Salt and pepper

1 tablespoon chopped fresh parsley

To make the salad, heap cooked rice in the middle of a serving dish, making a hole in the middle. Arrange the other salad ingredients nicely around it or over it.

To make the vinaigrette, combine all the ingredients. Pour the vinaigrette into the hole in the center of the platter. Garnish with parsley before serving.

◆ *4 to 6 servings*

Avocado Salad

Ensalada de Paltas ◆ *Argentina*

This salad is a wonderfully crisp side for hamburgers or chicken. For a chunkier texture I mash the avocados lightly.   —Lilly

2 ripe avocados, pitted
 and cut in half
1 teaspoon lime juice
2 tomatoes, finely chopped
½ cup chopped green onions

2 teaspoons chopped jalapeño
 peppers
¼ teaspoon garlic powder
Salt and pepper

Carefully scoop out the fruit from the avocados and reserve the skin of the 4 half shells intact. Lightly mash the fruit with a fork to keep a chunky texture. Add lime juice, tomatoes, green onions, and jalapeño peppers. Add the garlic powder, and salt and pepper to taste. Blend well. Spoon the avocado mixture into the reserved half shells and serve immediately.

◆ *4 servings*

Garbanzo Salad

Ensalada de Garbanzos ◆ *Spain*

Garbanzo is the Spanish word for "chickpea." This salad is best if made a day ahead.   —Nohemi

1 can (15 ounces) chickpeas,
   drained
¾ cup chopped celery
1 garlic clove, chopped
½ cup chopped red pimientos

2 tablespoons olive oil
3 green onions, chopped
2 tablespoons balsamic vinegar
½ cup sliced black or green olives
Salt and pepper

Combine all the ingredients in a salad bowl, adding salt and pepper to taste. Mix well and cover. Marinate for about 24 hours in the refrigerator before serving.

◆ *4 to 6 servings*

Cabbage Salad

Ensalada de Repollo ◆ *Argentina*

2 cups shredded cabbage

1 cup fresh diced tomatoes

1 cup diced Golden Delicious
apples

½ cup crumbled blue cheese

2 tablespoons fresh lemon juice

2 tablespoons olive oil

1 tablespoon chopped fresh parsley

½ teaspoon salt

Pinch of pepper

Mix all the ingredients together and refrigerate for 1 hour before serving.

◆ *4 to 6 servings*

Rice Salad

Ensalada Fría de Arroz ◆ *Spain*

1 cup rice

Salt

4 medium tomatoes, peeled
    and cut into small pieces

6 ounces fresh mushrooms, sliced

Juice of 1 lemon

1 can (4 ounces) pimientos,
    chopped

2 tablespoons chopped fresh
    parsley

2 tablespoons wine vinegar

6 tablespoons olive oil

1 hard-boiled egg, chopped

In a pan bring 4 cups of water to a boil. Add rice and stir a few times to keep it from sticking. Let it boil over medium heat for about 12 to 15 minutes or until the rice is tender. Drain and rinse under cold water. Lightly salt the tomato pieces and reserve. Put the mushroom slices in water with half of the lemon juice. Rinse, then stir in the other half of the lemon juice, mixing well to prevent the mushrooms from turning black. In a bowl, mix the salted tomatoes, mushrooms, pimientos, and parsley. Add the wine vinegar and olive oil. Stir entire mixture into the rice. Garnish with the hard-boiled egg before serving.

◆ *4 to 6 servings*

Green Salad
with Grapefruit Vinaigrette

ENSALADA VERDE CON VINAGRETA DE POMELOS ◆ *Argentina*

Salad

1 bag (10 ounces) ready-to-use
    fresh spinach
2 large heads Belgian endive,
    cut into pieces

1 bunch of radishes, trimmed
    and thinly sliced
2 avocados, peeled, pitted,
    and sliced

Vinaigrette

2 tablespoons balsamic vinegar
6 tablespoons olive oil
1½ teaspoons sugar

2 grapefruits, peeled, seeded,
    and sliced into rounds
Salt and pepper

To make the salad, combine spinach leaves, endive, and radishes in a
large bowl.

To make the vinaigrette, place vinegar in a small bowl and gradually mix
in oil. Add sugar and grapefruit. Season with salt and pepper to taste.
Pour vinaigrette over salad and toss. Top with avocado slices and serve.

◆ *4 to 6 servings*

Side Dishes

Nohemi's Croquets

CROQUETAS ◆ *Spain*

These tasty croquets can be served as appetizers or as side dishes. I still remember that when I was really young I watched Mamá making the shape of the croquets after they were coated with the bread crumbs. She always let me help her shape them, which was the fun part.   —Nohemi

2 tablespoons olive oil

3 tablespoons butter

5 tablespoons flour

2¾ cups milk

1 cup chopped cooked fish, shrimp, chicken, or ham

2 eggs

Bread crumbs to coat

Vegetable oil

In a skillet heat olive oil and butter over medium heat. Add flour, stirring with a wooden spoon. Add milk, a little at a time, stirring until the sauce becomes thick. Stir the chopped meat or fish of your choice into the sauce and pour into a 9 × 13-inch pan. Cool for at least 2 hours. Spoon a heaping amount of the cooled mixture in your hand and form into 1½-inch balls. Then shape each ball in the palm of your hand into the shape of 2 cones placed top-to-top. Beat the 2 eggs. Coat each croquet with bread crumbs, dip into the beaten eggs, and coat with bread crumbs once more. Pour oil into a deep fryer to a depth of 2 to 3 inches. Heat oil to 350°F. Fry the croquets a few at a time until golden. Remove and drain on paper towels.

◆ *4 to 6 servings*

Baked Corn Pudding

Puré de Maíz • *Colombia*

This pudding may be served with meat or chicken.   —Nora

6 tablespoons butter

1 large onion, chopped

1 garlic clove, minced

½ green bell pepper, seeded
   and chopped

½ red bell pepper, seeded
   and chopped

½ jalapeño or other hot pepper,
   seeded and chopped

¼ cup flour

Salt and pepper

2 cans (28 ounces)
   cream-style corn

6 eggs, slightly beaten

2 cups milk

Preheat oven to 350°F. Melt the butter in a skillet at medium heat. Add onion, garlic, and all of the peppers. Cook, stirring until vegetables are tender. Stir in flour and salt and pepper to taste, until mixture is bubbly. Remove from heat. Add corn, eggs, and milk, stirring the entire time until the mixture is well blended. Pour the corn mixture into a shallow, buttered bowl or baking dish. Bake for 55 minutes or until center is set.

◆ *4 to 6 servings*

Corn Crepes

CANELONES DE CHOCLO   ◆   *Argentina*

Crepes

2 eggs at room temperature

¾ cup milk

⅔ cup beer

1 cup flour

⅓ teaspoon salt

2 tablespoons oil or butter

Filling

4 tablespoons butter

1 onion, chopped

2 tablespoons flour

1 to 1½ cups hot half-and-half

2 cans (28 ounces) corn, drained

Salt and pepper

Assembly

1 cup fresh grated Parmesan or
   Romano cheese

1 cup prepared pasta sauce with
   mushrooms

To make the crepes, place the eggs, milk, and beer in a blender or food processor and add the flour and salt. Blend for 2 minutes and then scrape down the sides. Blend for 1 more minute or until the mixture is smooth. Add the oil or butter. Cover and refrigerate for at least 2 hours. Remove from the refrigerator. Heat an oiled crepe pan to medium hot. Pour in 2 tablespoons of batter for each crepe. Tip and turn the pan until batter covers the bottom. Cook until the bottom appears dry. Turn with the spatula and cook the other side until golden brown. Stack crepes with a piece of wax paper in between each crepe.

To make the filling, melt the butter in a skillet and sauté the onion. Add the flour and very slowly the hot half-and-half. Stir constantly until a creamy mixture forms. Add the corn and season with salt and pepper to taste. Simmer for 8 minutes at low heat. Stir in half of the Parmesan or Romano cheese. If the mixture is too thick you can add a little more half-and-half or milk. Remove from heat.

To assemble the dish, bring the stack of crepes to a clean surface. Spread 2 tablespoons of the corn mixture in each crepe and roll. Keep stuffing and rolling the crepes until finished. In a baking dish, put some butter or oil. Arrange the crepes side by side. Pour the pasta sauce on top. Sprinkle with the remaining Parmesan or Romano cheese. Bake for 30 minutes at 350°F.

◆ *4 to 6 servings*

Braised Peas and Corn with Prosciutto

Arvejas y Choclo a la Crema con Jamón Crudo ◆ *Peru*

2 tablespoons butter
¼ cup finely chopped onion
2 cups fresh sugar snap peas,
    unshelled
1 cup fresh corn kernels

¼ cup light cream
2 ounces prosciutto, cut into strips
1 tablespoon fresh grated
    Parmesan cheese
Salt and pepper

In a heavy skillet, melt the butter over moderate heat. Sauté the onion for 3 minutes, stirring frequently until they are soft. Stir in the green peas and corn. Simmer for 7 minutes. Add the cream and the strips of prosciutto and cook for 2 more minutes. Add the Parmesan cheese, and salt and pepper to taste. Cook until peas and corn are tender.

◆ *4 to 6 servings*

Peas with Ham

Guisantes con Jamón ◆ *Spain*

When I was a young girl, Mamá had a vegetable garden. My brother, my sister, and I were expected to help weed the garden and pick the vegetables when they were ripe. One Saturday afternoon Mamá sent me out to pick peas so that she could make them for dinner. As I shelled the sweet little peas I popped some into my mouth. They were delicious! Before I knew it, I had eaten all the peas from the garden and there were none left for dinner. Mamá was not happy with me!   —Noemi

¼ cup olive oil

1 large onion, chopped

1 large carrot, grated

¼ pound cooked ham, diced

2 pounds (2 cups) cooked peas

Salt and pepper

Heat the oil and sauté onion and carrot. When onion is a golden color, add ham. Cook for 10 minutes until browned, then stir in the peas. Season with salt and pepper to taste before serving.

◆ *4 to 6 servings*

Country Beans

Garbanzos del Campo ◆ *Peru*

Chickpeas were brought to South America by the Spanish. They were welcomed in every kitchen and have been widely used ever since. This is a simple recipe for a side dish of these delightful beans.   —Ana

1 cup chickpeas, soaked for 4 hours	½ cup olive oil
	1 garlic clove, peeled
1 teaspoon salt	Salt

Drain the chickpeas. Cover with fresh water and simmer for 30 minutes. Add the salt and continue cooking until they are tender, about 1 hour. Drain and cool. Heat the olive oil in a skillet and sauté the chickpeas with the garlic until they are browned. Drain on paper towels and sprinkle with salt to taste.

◆ *4 to 6 servings*

Green Beans with Ham and Cream

Chauchas con Jamón y Crema ◆ *Argentina*

This is a great side dish for grilled meat or chicken, like the Glazed Ham on page 140 or the Filet Mignon with Maitre de Hotel Butter on page 164.   —Lilly

½ pound fresh green beans

4 tablespoons butter

2 garlic cloves, peeled

1 thick ham steak, cut into
fine strips

Salt and pepper

1 cup cream

3 tablespoons fresh grated
Parmesan cheese

Wash the beans. Boil in salty water, until they are just a little tender. Remove and drain. In a skillet, melt the butter and sauté the garlic cloves for just a minute. Make sure you don't brown the garlic. Turn the heat to low. Add the beans and ham to the skillet. Mix well. Cook for about 8 minutes, allowing the flavors to blend. Season with salt and pepper to taste. Add the cream and Parmesan cheese. Cook at a very low temperature for another 3 minutes.

◆ *4 to 6 servings*

Lemon Green Beans

CHAUCHAS CON LIMÓN ◆ *Colombia*

2 pounds fresh green beans,
   cut in half
1 tablespoon chopped fresh parsley
1 garlic clove, chopped
¼ cup olive oil

2 tablespoons chopped almonds
Salt and pepper
2 tablespoons butter
1 tablespoon fresh lemon juice

Cook beans in boiling salted water, until they are a little tender. Do not over-cook. Drain in a colander and reserve. In a small bowl, blend parsley with garlic, olive oil, and almonds. Add salt and pepper to taste. Mix well. In a saucepan melt butter, add the beans and toss in the hot butter to coat. Let the beans cool a little bit. Add the parsley-garlic mixture. Add the lemon juice and mix well.

◆ *4 to 6 servings*

Lima Beans with Clams

Habas con Chirlas ◆ *Spain*

1 tablespoon olive oil

1 large onion, quartered and sliced
   crosswise into ¼-inch pieces

2 bay leaves

⅓ cup dry white wine

2 packages (40 ounces) frozen
   baby lima beans, thawed

3 garlic cloves, minced

Salt

2 dozen small clams, scrubbed

3 large tomatoes, cut into chunks

¼ cup chopped fresh parsley

In a large, deep skillet, heat oil over medium heat. Add onion and bay
leaves and sauté until the onion is golden. Add white wine and simmer
for 2 minutes. Add lima beans and minced garlic. Season with salt to taste.
Arrange clams on top of lima beans. Increase the heat to medium high.
Cover and cook until clams open, about 8 minutes. Place clams in a bowl.
Remove half of the clams from the shells and stir into the beans. Mix tomatoes and parsley into beans. Pour into serving dish. Top with remaining
clams in their shells before serving.

◆ *4 to 6 servings*

AT THE FAIR

by Noemi

I remember that when I was a young girl, Mamá and her friends had an idea to set up a food cart and take it to all the local county fairs to sell Spanish food. The specialty food that the cart would feature was *empanadas,* which are similar to American turnovers. *Empanadas* are common to all four countries—Spain, Peru, Colombia, and Argentina.

Turnovers (empanadas)

In Spain they are called *empanadillas*. They originated in Spain, whose foods were influenced by the Moors from the Middle East. Spanish conquerors spread the dish to the other countries and today one can find *empanadas* of different varieties in all the Spanish-speaking countries. *Empanadas* are often stuffed with meat and various vegetables. Nohemi, Ana, Nora, and Lilly intended to sell them on a cart named *Las Amigas*, which means "Friends." Eventually, they abandoned the idea. Traveling to the local fairs and selling food to turn a profit is very hard work, especially since they were raising young children. However, I have no doubt that *Las Amigas* would have been successful had they decided to give the venture a try. Imagine going to a fair and instead of having a regular hot dog, French fries, and Coke, you could have a tasty bit of delicious Spanish food, made by four women who offered it to you because they wanted to share their friendship and food with everyone. The following three recipes are for *empanadas* that use different ingredients.

Pork-Filled Turnovers

Pastelitos Rellenos de Cerdo ◆ *Colombia*

Pastry

2 cups flour

1 teaspoon salt

½ cup butter

½ teaspoon fresh lemon juice

½ cup lukewarm water

Filling

½ pound ground pork

1 large onion, grated

1 hard-boiled egg, finely chopped

½ cup finely chopped ham

3 tablespoons golden raisins

Salt and pepper

Dash of oregano

Assembly

Vegetable oil

To make the pastry, sift the flour and salt into a large bowl. Cut the butter into small pieces and rub into the flour with fingertips to form a coarse meal. Mix the lemon juice with water. Using a fork, stir in the water quickly to make a soft dough. Roll into a ball and refrigerate, covered with wax paper, for at least 30 minutes. Roll out the pastry on a floured surface to a thickness of ⅛ inch and cut into rounds or circles with a cookie cutter or something similar.

To make the filling, coat the bottom of a skillet with oil, then fry the ground pork and onion. Add the hard-boiled egg, ham, and raisins. Cook for about 15 minutes. Season with salt and pepper to taste, and the oregano. Mix well.

To assemble the turnover, put 1 tablespoon of the filling in each pastry circle, fold the pastry in half to make a turnover, and seal the edges by pressing with the tines of a fork. Pour enough vegetable oil in a fryer or saucepan to reach a depth of 2 to 3 inches. Heat to 350°F. Fry the turnovers, a few at a time, until they are golden on both sides. Drain on paper towels.

◆ *4 to 6 servings*

Spanish Turnovers

Empanadillas Españolas ◆ *Spain*

You can make the turnovers smaller than this recipe calls for and serve them as appetizers. I remember that Mamá used a glass to cut the circles. After folding the circles in half over the filling, she would let me seal the edges with my fingers. She would give my younger brothers and sisters pieces of the dough to play with and keep them occupied while she cooked.
—Nohemi

Pastry

3 tablespoons olive oil
1 cup water
½ cup dry white wine

2½ cups flour
Salt

Filling

1 small onion, chopped
1 tablespoon olive oil
3 tablespoons thick tomato sauce
    or paste
1 hard-boiled egg, chopped
Pinch of paprika

Pinch of chopped fresh parsley
Pinch of nutmeg
Salt and pepper
Cooked ham, chicken, ground
    meat, fish, or canned tuna,
    chopped

Assembly

Vegetable oil

To make the pastry, heat oil, water, and white wine in a small saucepan. In a mixing bowl, mix flour and salt to taste. Pour the warm water mixture over the flour mixture and stir with a spoon. When it becomes hard to stir, turn the mixture out onto a floured counter and mix well, kneading for about 1 to 2 minutes. Shape into a ball, cover, and let rest for 2 hours.

To make the filling, sauté the onion in skillet with the oil. Mix in tomato sauce, hard-boiled egg, spices, and meat or fish of your choice.

To assemble the turnovers, on a floured surface, roll the dough out with a rolling pin to a thickness of $\frac{1}{8}$ inch. Cut out circles 3 inches wide. Fill circles in the center with the filling and fold over to make half moons. Seal the edges. Pour oil into a deep fryer or pan to depth of 2 or 3 inches. Heat oil to 350°F. Deep fry until golden and drain on paper towels.

◆ *4 to 6 servings*

Colombian Turnovers

Empanadas a la Santa Fe ◆ *Colombia*

Pastry

1¼ cups boiling water

1 cup vegetable shortening

1 teaspoon salt

4½ cups flour

Filling

1½ pounds lean ground beef

4 cups diced, cooked potatoes

1 cup finely chopped onions

1 garlic clove, chopped

2 teaspoons salt

Pepper

Assembly

Vegetable oil

To make the pastry, combine boiling water, shortening, and salt in a bowl. Stir until shortening melts. Add flour and stir. Gather into a ball. Cover with plastic wrap and refrigerate for 1 hour.

To make the filling, in a large bowl, combine all the ingredients.

To assemble the turnovers, divide the pastry into 8 parts. On a floured board roll each part out to make a 9-inch circle. Place 1 heaping cupful of filling into the center of each pastry round. Fold pastry over filling and seal. Place on an ungreased baking sheet. With a fork, press edges together and pierce tops. Fill a pan or deep fryer to a depth of 2 to 3 inches and heat oil to 350°F. Fry until crispy on the outside and serve.

◆ *4 to 6 servings*

Lentils with Garlic

LENTEJAS GUISADAS ◆ *Spain*

I spent the summer of my eighth year staying with my family in Spain. My great-aunt Sira used to serve the most delicious lentils for lunch. In Spain, lunch is often the largest meal of the day and consists of several courses. I will never forget those tasty lentils.   —Noemi

2 cups lentils

1 bay leaf

½ onion, cut in half

2 garlic cloves

1 onion, chopped

½ cup olive oil

1 ripe tomato, peeled and chopped

1 teaspoon paprika

Salt and pepper

2 sprigs of parsley

Soak lentils in water overnight. Drain. In a pan, place the lentils, bay leaf, ½ onion, and 1 of the garlic cloves (unpeeled). Cover with water. Cover and bring to a boil. Simmer for 1½ hours. In a skillet over medium heat, sauté the chopped onion in oil until golden, about 8 minutes. Add the tomato and continue cooking another 3 to 4 minutes. With the skillet off the heat, add paprika and stir. Add mixture to the lentils. Crush the other (peeled) garlic clove and add salt and pepper to it. Dilute it with 3 to 4 tablespoons of the lentil broth and pour over the lentils. Stir well and bring to a soft boil for about 10 minutes. Take out the bay leaf and unpeeled garlic clove and garnish with parsley before serving.

◆ *4 to 6 servings*

Nohemi's nieces (and Noemi's cousins) Berta and Laura in Spain wearing traditional flamenco costumes

Glorious Plantains

Plátanos en Gloria • *Colombia*

3 ripe plantains, peeled and sliced
   diagonally ¼-inch thick
4 tablespoons butter
Salt

¼ pound mild cheese, grated
½ to 1 cup cream
¼ cup fresh grated Parmesan
   cheese

Preheat oven to 350°F. In a skillet, fry plantain slices lightly in butter until browned on both sides. Drain on paper towels and sprinkle with salt to taste. In a buttered casserole, arrange alternate layers of plantains and grated cheese, finishing with a cheese layer. Pour cream over top until it shows through the top layer of cheese. Sprinkle with Parmesan cheese. Bake until firm but not dry, about 45 minutes.

• *4 to 6 servings*

Banana Fritters

Buñuelos de Banana ◆ *Peru*

This recipe makes a delicious side dish for ham or pork or you can even serve it as a dessert. Buñuelos are typically made for special holidays like Christmas and Easter. They also can be served with syrup or honey.
    —Ana

¾ cup flour

3 tablespoons sugar

1 teaspoon baking powder

⅛ teaspoon cinnamon

2 eggs

½ cup milk

¾ cup sliced bananas

¼ cup olive oil

Confectioners' sugar

In a large bowl, blend flour, sugar, baking powder, and cinnamon. In another bowl, beat eggs, milk, and bananas. Stir in the flour mixture, blending to make a smooth batter. Pour oil into a heavy skillet and heat over medium heat to 350°F. Drop batter by tablespoons in the hot oil. Cook until the fritters are golden brown on both sides. Arrange on a dish lined with paper towels to absorb the oil. Dust with confectioners' sugar before serving.

◆ *4 to 6 servings*

Zucchini with Corn and Peppers

CALABACITAS CON MAIZ Y AJIES • *Colombia*

This side is a bright addition to any meal with its array of red, green, and yellow bell peppers. —Nora

3 tablespoons bacon drippings

2 pounds zucchini, cubed

1½ cups fresh corn kernels, or 1 package (10 ounces) frozen corn, thawed

1 red bell pepper, seeded and chopped

1 green bell pepper, seeded and chopped

1 yellow bell pepper, seeded and chopped

Salt and pepper

In a skillet over high heat, melt the bacon drippings. Add zucchini, corn, and all the peppers. Cook, stirring often, until all the liquid from the vegetables has evaporated and they are tender and crispy. Add salt and pepper to taste before serving.

• *4 to 6 servings*

Zucchini Pisto

Pisto de Calabacín ◆ *Spain*

Growing up, this was one of my favorite dishes. I can still remember the distinctive flavor of the zucchini stronger than all the other vegetables.   —Nohemi

¼ cup olive oil

1 large onion, chopped

2 green bell peppers, seeded and
    chopped

2 potatoes, peeled and finely sliced

1 pound zucchini, chopped

1 pound ripe tomatoes, peeled
    and chopped

1 tablespoon sugar

Salt

Put oil in a saucepan. Sauté onion, stirring, about 5 minutes. Add peppers and potatoes. Cook 3 to 4 minutes before adding the zucchini. Add tomatoes, sugar, and salt to taste and cook at low heat for 30 minutes, stirring occasionally.

◆ *4 to 6 servings*

Peasant Eggplant

BERENJENAS A LA CRIOLLA ◆ *Peru*

2 medium eggplants, peeled and
   cut into ½-inch slices

3 tablespoons olive oil

1 medium onion, chopped

1 green bell pepper, seeded
   and finely chopped

1 yellow bell pepper, seeded
   and finely chopped

1 red bell pepper, seeded and finely
   chopped

2 garlic cloves, minced

2 cups canned crushed tomatoes

1 bay leaf

1 teaspoon dry oregano

½ cup red wine

Salt and pepper

1 cup shredded mozzarella cheese

1 tablespoon chopped fresh parsley

Sprinkle the eggplant slices with salt on both sides. In a skillet or saucepan
bring 2 cups water to a boil. Add the eggplant slices and blanche for 2 minutes or until slightly tender. Drain in a colander and reserve. In a heavy
skillet, heat the olive oil. Add onion and all peppers. Add garlic and tomatoes. Add the bay leaf and oregano. Cook until the mixture is soft, at low
heat. Add wine. Simmer for 2 more minutes. Season with salt and pepper to
taste. Preheat oven to 350°F. Grease a square baking dish. Cover the bottom with a fine layer of tomato mixture. Arrange a layer of eggplant slices
on top. Top with tomato mixture and sprinkle with mozzarella cheese. Continue the layering of eggplant, tomatoes, and cheese. Top the last layer of
the eggplant with the remaining tomatoes and cheese. Sprinkle parsley on
top. Bake for 20 minutes or until it is hot and bubbly.

◆ *4 to 6 servings*

Tasty Cauliflower

Coliflor Sabrosa ◆ *Argentina*

Sauce

1 to 1½ cups half-and-half

3 tablespoons butter

2 tablespoons flour

1 egg yolk

Cauliflower

1 cauliflower

1 tablespoon olive oil

Salt

2 green onions, chopped

1 cup shredded Cheddar cheese

To make the sauce, heat up the half-and-half in a microwave oven. In a saucepan, melt the butter, and add the flour to form a paste. Add the hot half-and-half, stirring constantly to avoid lumps. Cook for about 3 minutes at low heat. Add the egg yolk and cook for another 5 minutes.

To prepare the cauliflower, separate the florets into small pieces and boil in salted water until they are a little tender. Make sure you don't overcook. Drain in a colander and reserve. In a skillet, heat olive oil and sauté green onions. Add cauliflower pieces. Mix well. Preheat oven to 350°F. Arrange a layer of cauliflower in a buttered baking dish. Top with a little of the sauce. Sprinkle some of the Cheddar cheese on top. Keep going in this manner, with a layer of cauliflower, sauce, then cheese. Bake for 15 minutes or until the cheese is hot and bubbly.

◆ *4 to 6 servings*

Cauliflower with White Sauce

COLIFLOR CON BECHAMEL ◆ *Spain*

Juice of ½ lemon

1 medium cauliflower,
   cut into small florets

2 tablespoons olive oil

2 tablespoons flour

Salt and pepper

2 cups milk

½ cup shredded Swiss cheese

In a saucepan with enough water to cover the cauliflower add the lemon juice. Boil cauliflower until tender. Drain. Place in an ovenproof dish. Heat oil in a skillet. Add flour, and salt and pepper to taste, and stir until no lumps remain. Stirring constantly, add the milk little by little. Cook over medium heat for 5 minutes. Pour over cauliflower. Sprinkle cheese on top and broil until brown, about 10 minutes.

◆ *4 to 6 servings*

Onion Tart

Tarta de Cebolla ◆ *Argentina*

2 cups plus 3 tablespoons flour

1 teaspoon salt

10 tablespoons butter, very cold

4 to 6 tablespoons ice water

1 pound dried beans

3 tablespoons oil

6 cups thinly sliced onions

½ cup chopped jalapeño
   or chili peppers

3 tablespoons flour

3 eggs

2 cups half-and-half

1 teaspoon salt

Dash of pepper

¾ cup shredded Swiss cheese

Mix flour and salt in medium bowl. Cut in butter until mixture resembles coarse crumbs. Gradually stir in ice water. Gather into a ball and knead 3 or 4 times. Refrigerate, wrapped in plastic, for 2 hours. Heat oven to 370°F. Roll pastry out. Place into a pie pan. Pierce the bottom of the pastry in several places with a fork. Line pastry with aluminum foil. Fill with the dry beans. Bake until pastry is set, about 10 minutes. Remove foil and beans (beans are not used in tart). Heat oil in a skillet. Stir in onions and hot peppers. Cook until onions are golden. Stir in flour. Cook mixture. Whisk eggs lightly in a large bowl. Stir in half-and-half. Stir in onion mixture. Season with salt and pepper. Carefully pour mixture into pastry shell. Sprinkle the Swiss cheese on top. Bake for 30 minutes.

◆ *4 to 6 servings*

Chickpeas with Garlic

Garbanzos Saltados al Ajo ◆ *Colombia*

1 pound (2 cups) dried chickpeas,
    soaked for 4 hours or overnight
½ cup olive oil

3 garlic cloves, chopped
1 tablespoon chopped fresh parsley
1 teaspoon dried basil

Drain chickpeas, cover with fresh water and cook for 1 hour. When they are tender, drain and reserve. Heat olive oil in a skillet and sauté chickpeas. Add garlic, parsley, and basil. Cook until chickpeas are browned, stirring occasionally.

◆ *4 to 6 servings*

Spinach au Gratin

ESPINACAS CON BECHAMEL ◆ *Spain*

3 packages (30 ounces) frozen
  chopped spinach, thawed
5 tablespoons butter
Salt and pepper
2 tablespoons flour

½ cup whipping cream
½ cup milk
Pinch of ground nutmeg
⅔ cup fresh grated Romano cheese

Preheat oven to 375°F. Grease an 8 × 9-inch glass baking dish. Squeeze the spinach very dry. Melt 3 tablespoons of the butter in a skillet over medium heat. Add spinach and sauté 4 minutes. Season with salt and pepper to taste. Spread over the prepared baking dish. Over medium heat, melt the remaining 2 tablespoons of butter. Add flour and whisk 2 minutes. Do not brown. Gradually add cream, then milk, whisking until the mixture is smooth, about 7 minutes. Add the nutmeg and season with salt and pepper to taste. Spoon sauce over spinach and sprinkle Romano cheese on top. Bake until cheese is golden, about 15 minutes.

◆ *4 to 6 servings*

Spinach Soufflé

SOUFFLE DE ESPINACAS • *Peru*

5 tablespoons butter

1 tablespoon chopped green onions

¾ cup frozen chopped spinach, thawed

Dash of nutmeg

3 tablespoons flour

1 cup half-and-half

Salt and pepper

4 eggs, separated

¼ teaspoon cream of tartar

1 tablespoon fresh grated Parmesan cheese

Melt 1 tablespoon of the butter in a small pan. Sauté the green onions until tender. Add spinach. Cook a few minutes to remove moisture. Add nutmeg. Set aside. Melt the remaining 4 tablespoons of butter in a saucepan. Stir in flour. Cook for several minutes. Add the half-and-half all at once. Add salt and pepper to taste. Cook and stir over medium heat until sauce thickens. Stir in spinach mixture. Cool sauce, then add egg yolks. Mix well. Preheat oven to 375°F. In a medium-sized bowl beat the egg whites until frothy. Beat in the cream of tartar. Continue beating until soft peaks form. Stir ¼ of the egg whites into the spinach sauce. Gently fold in the remaining whites. Butter a 2-quart soufflé dish and dust with the Parmesan cheese. Pour the mixture into the prepared dish. Bake for 30 minutes. The soufflé is done when it is golden, puffed, and a little dry.

• 4 to 6 servings

Stuffed Tomatoes

Tomates Rellenos ◆ *Argentina*

6 whole tomatoes

1 can (6 ounces) tuna fish

½ cup cooked rice

1 cup mayonnaise

1 tablespoon fresh lemon juice

Salt and pepper

1 teaspoon chopped fresh parsley

Cut off tomato stems. Scoop out pulp. Turn tomatoes upside down to drain. Combine tuna, rice, mayonnaise, and lemon juice. Mix well. Salt and pepper the tomatoes. Fill with the mixture. Garnish with the parsley before serving.

◆ *4 to 6 servings*

Marinated Tomatoes

TOMATES MARINADOS ◆ *Argentina*

This salad is lovely on its own or as a side dish for meat, such as the Orange Pork Loin recipe on page 135.   —Lilly

3 large tomatoes, cut into
   ½-inch slices

⅓ cup olive oil

¼ cup balsamic vinegar

¼ cup chopped green onions

2 tablespoons chopped
   fresh parsley

1 garlic clove, minced

1 teaspoon salt

1 teaspoon oregano

Dash of pepper

½ cup crumbled feta cheese

Arrange tomatoes in a single layer in a shallow dish. Combine oil and remaining ingredients, except cheese, in a medium bowl, stirring to blend. Spoon dressing over tomatoes. Cover and marinate in refrigerator 3 hours. When ready to serve, mix all the ingredients again and top with the feta cheese.

◆ *4 to 6 servings*

Fried Rice Balls with Cheese

ALMÓNDIGAS DE ARROZ RELLENAS CON QUESO ◆ *Peru*

Rice is one of the main dishes in the Peruvian kitchen. Eaten by most families twice a day, rice is a good accompaniment to chicken, fish, or meat.   —Ana

2 tablespoons olive oil

2 green onions, finely chopped

½ jalapeño pepper, seeded
   and chopped

½ green bell pepper, seeded
   and chopped

½ red bell pepper, seeded
   and chopped

2 garlic cloves, minced

1 cup cooked rice

3 tablespoons fresh grated
   Parmesan cheese

2 eggs, slightly beaten

Salt and pepper

4 ounces mozzarella cheese,
   cut into small cubes

¾ cup fine dried bread crumbs

Heat olive oil in a skillet. Add green onions, all peppers, and garlic. Cook until vegetables are soft. Add cooked rice, Parmesan cheese, and eggs. Mix well. Add salt and pepper to taste. Scoop up 1 tablespoon of the rice mixture in a spoon. Place a cube of Mozzarella cheese in the middle and top with another spoonful of rice mixture. Press the 2 spoons together or use your hands to shape a ball. Roll the balls in bread crumbs and place on wax paper. Shape the remaining balls and refrigerate for 30 minutes. Heat 2 to 3 inches of oil in a heavy skillet to 350°F. Fry the balls, 3 or 4 at a time, for about 5 minutes or until they are golden and the cheese has melted. Transfer to a baking dish. Cover with paper towels and drain well before serving.

◆ *4 to 6 servings*

Meat and Rice Stuffed Green Peppers

PIMIENTOS RELLENOS DE CARNE Y ARROZ ◆ *Spain*

Saffron is a spice that is sold in either threads or powder. The threads are a more pure form of this spice. The region of La Mancha in Spain is the source of the finest quality saffron. Because of its rarity and the work it takes to hand pick it, it is considered one of the world's most highly valued spices. Mixed in with a variety of chicken and rice dishes, saffron gives a food a yellow color, a spicy aroma, and a delicious taste. It is the mainstay ingredient of the famous Spanish *paella*. It is possible to find this rare spice in gourmet and grocery stores in metropolitan areas, as well as on the Internet.   —Noemi

6 medium green bell peppers

6 tablespoons rice

1 ½ cups ground beef

1 small garlic clove, chopped

1 teaspoon chopped fresh parsley

Salt

¼ cup olive oil

1 medium onion, chopped

1 tablespoon flour

Pinch of powdered saffron

2 cubes beef bouillon

Cut the tops off of the peppers and reserve. Throw out seeds. Place a tablespoon of raw rice in each pepper cup. In a small bowl, mix the ground meat, garlic, parsley, and salt to taste. Stuff the peppers with the mixture. Cover the cups with the pepper tops. Heat oil in a large saucepan. Sauté onion for 7 minutes. Add flour and stir. Add saffron and 3 to 4 cups of water, stirring constantly. Add bouillon cubes, stir, and cook for 3 minutes. Place the stuffed peppers in the pan and add more water to cover the peppers halfway up. Cover the pan. Simmer for 50 minutes or until the peppers are done.

◆ *6 servings*

Lima Rice

ARROZ DE LIMA ◆ *Peru*

1 ½ cups long-grain rice

1 cup finely chopped ham

¾ cup cream

3 hard-boiled eggs, chopped

½ cup chopped roasted peppers

¼ cup chopped fresh parsley

Salt and pepper

2 tomatoes, cut into thick rounds

Dash of oregano

1 cup shredded mozzarella cheese

Bring 8 cups of salted water to a boil. Add rice. Cover pan and cook rice until it is tender, 15 to 20 minutes. Drain and let cool for 5 minutes. Pour rice into a medium bowl. Add ham, cream, eggs, peppers, and parsley. Blend all together. Add salt and pepper to taste. Preheat oven to 350°F. Grease a baking dish with a little butter or oil and fill with the rice mixture. Arrange tomato rounds on top. Add a little salt, pepper, and oregano. Sprinkle mozzarella cheese on top of the tomatoes. Bake for 15 minutes or until the cheese is melted.

◆ *4 to 6 servings*

Kidney Beans with Rice

Judias Pintas con Arroz • *Spain*

1 pound (2 cups) dried
   kidney beans
1 medium onion, peeled
   and cut in half
1 bay leaf
1 garlic clove, peeled
2½ cups rice
¼ cup olive oil

1 medium onion, peeled
   and chopped
1 garlic clove, chopped
1 tablespoon flour
1 teaspoon paprika
2 tablespoons butter
Salt

In a large pan, cover beans with water. Cover and bring to a boil. Drain, reserving liquid, and cover beans with cold water again. Add onion that is cut in half, bay leaf, and garlic clove. Boil over low heat, pouring about ¼ cup of cold water into beans 3 times during this process to stop them from boiling too hard. Cook about 2½ hours or until tender. In the meantime, make the rice. In a pan, bring a large amount of water to a boil and add rice. Stir and boil hard about 15 minutes. Drain, rinse under cold water, and drain again in a colander. Place in a pan and keep warm over low heat. Heat oil in a skillet and add chopped onion and garlic. Sauté until golden. Add flour and lightly brown. Add paprika and 3 to 4 tablespoons of the reserved bean juice. Stir and pour over the cooked beans. Add butter and salt to the rice. Pour the rice onto a serving plate, making a hole in the center. Remove bay leaf and whole garlic clove from beans and pour into the center of the rice.

◆ *4 to 6 servings*

Raisin and Almond Rice

Arroz con Almendras y Pasas de Uvas • *Peru*

3 tablespoons butter

¼ cup sliced almonds

1 small onion, chopped

⅓ cup golden raisins

1½ cups long-grain rice

3 cups boiling chicken stock

Salt and pepper

Melt butter. Add almonds and fry over medium heat, stirring until they are golden brown. Remove almonds to a plate covered with paper towels and set aside. Add onions to the pan and sauté until soft. Stir in raisins and rice and sauté until the rice looks slightly translucent, 2 or 3 minutes. Add the hot stock. Bring to a boil, then cover the pan and steam over low heat until the rice is tender and all the stock has been absorbed. Season with salt and pepper to taste. Add the almonds and fluff rice with a fork before serving.

• *4 to 6 servings*

Spanish Rice

Paella ◆ *Spain*

Paella is frequently the dish that comes to mind when one thinks of Spanish food. Often served with a variety of seafood and chicken, this rice dish achieves its savory flavor from the spice saffron. In addition to the flavor, saffron gives the rice its yellow coloring. Saffron used to be difficult to obtain in America, but now it can be found in gourmet shops, grocery stores, and the Internet. It comes in powder form and in threads that need to be ground. Growing up, *paella* was one of my brother Kris's favorite dishes. In addition to having it several times during the year, Mamá always made it especially for his birthday. Even now, as an adult, he still asks for *paella* for his birthday dinner.   —Noemi

½ cup olive oil

1 small onion, chopped

1 green bell pepper, seeded
   and chopped

½ chicken, cut into small pieces

2 small tomatoes, peeled
   and chopped

½ pound shrimp, washed,
   peeled, and deveined

½ pound small clams, washed

½ cup green peas

1 small squid,
   cut into rings

2 cups rice

1 small garlic clove

1 sprig of parsley

4 to 5 threads of saffron

Salt

1 can (4 ounces) pimientos

Heat ¼ cup of the oil in a skillet. Sauté onion for 5 minutes. Add green pepper and chicken. Stir and cook for 5 minutes, turning chicken until browned. Add tomatoes. Sauté 5 more minutes, stirring. Set aside. In a saucepan with cold salted water, cook peels from shrimp for a few minutes. In another saucepan with a little water, boil the clams just until they open. Discard the half empty shells of the clams. Reserve the rest. Through a fine colander pass the broth from the shrimp shells and the water from the clams. Reserve this seafood broth. In a round, flat, large skillet, heat the other ¼ cup of oil. Add the chicken-vegetable mixture, peas, squid, and rice. Mix and fry at medium heat for about 1 minute. Add salt to taste and stir in seafood broth. If there is not enough broth to make 4 cups, add water. Shake the skillet to spread the broth well. Cook over medium heat. In the meantime, in a garlic pestle, smash the small garlic clove, parsley sprig, and saffron with a little salt. Add 2 tablespoons of warm water to the garlic, mix, and pour over the rice. Shake the skillet to mix well. Add the shrimp, making a design over the rice. When the rice has almost absorbed the broth, about 20 minutes, add pimiento strips and the small clams, making a design with both over the rice.

◆ *4 to 6 servings*

*Ana enjoying
a plate of Nohemi's
Spanish Rice*
(paella)

Nohemi's Vegetable Bake

Budin de Verduras ◆ *Spain*

1 cup carrots, peeled and sliced
    into rounds
6 tablespoons butter
1 cup green peas
3 pounds spinach, chopped
    and cooked
2 eggs

3 tablespoons milk
2 tablespoons olive oil
2 tablespoons flour
2 cups milk
Salt
1 tablespoon tomato paste

Steam carrots until tender. Reserve some as rounds, chop the rest. Use some of the butter to grease an ovenproof, nonstick mold. Place some of the carrot rounds and some of the peas in the bottom of the mold, creating a design. Preheat oven to 350°F. Bring a kettle of water to a boil. Heat the rest of the butter in a skillet. Add the rest of the peas and the spinach and sauté. In a bowl, beat the eggs and add the 3 tablespoons of milk. Take the pan off the heat. Add the vegetables to the egg mixture and stir. Pour over the prepared pan, pressing a bit to take the air bubbles out. Place in a roasting pan and add enough hot water from the kettle to reach halfway up the pan. Bake for 1 hour. In the meantime, make the tomato sauce. In a skillet, heat oil and butter (the remaining butter after greasing the mold). Add flour, stirring. Add the 2 cups of milk a little at a time, stirring constantly. Add salt to taste and cook over medium heat, stirring, for 10 to 15 minutes. Add tomato paste and stir vigorously to mix well. Turn off the oven and open the door, leaving the baked vegetables in it for 8 minutes. Run a knife around the sides of the pan and turn it over onto a serving plate. Pour the tomato sauce over the vegetable bake before serving.

◆ *4 to 6 servings*

Vegetable Omelet

Tortilla de Verduras ◆ *Colombia*

1 tablespoon olive oil

4 large potatoes, peeled and cut
   into small chunks

2 carrots, peeled and sliced

2 garlic cloves, minced

2 small onions, peeled and
   cut into rings

4 artichokes, tough outer leaves
   removed, cut into
   8 thin slices

½ cauliflower, broken into florets

1 sprig of parsley, chopped

5 sprigs of marjoram, chopped

7 eggs

Salt and pepper

Heat olive oil in a skillet. Add all the vegetables, except the cauliflower, and cook for a few minutes. Then stir in the cauliflower florets. Cook for 3 to 4 minutes and remove. Drain and put aside. Clean the leaves of the parsley and marjoram. Beat the eggs and mix in the herbs and the cooked vegetables. Season with salt and pepper to taste and pour into the pan. Fry the *tortilla* on both sides until brown.

◆ *4 to 6 servings*

Omelet with Lamb Kidneys

TORTILLA DEL MONTE ◆ *Colombia*

2 tablespoons olive oil

3 medium potatoes, peeled
   and sliced

1 onion, sliced

8 ounces lamb kidneys, washed
   and cut into pieces

$3\frac{1}{2}$ ounces of mild ham, cubed

8 eggs

Salt and pepper

In a skillet, fry the potatoes and onions in 1 tablespoon of the oil until golden. In a separate pan, fry both lamb kidneys and ham briskly. Cover and simmer for 10 minutes. Remove and mix with the potato mixture. In a second pan, heat the remaining tablespoon of oil and add the mixture. Beat the eggs lightly without blending the yolks and whites. Add salt and pepper to taste and pour into the pan. Turn the omelet over to fry on both sides; it should be soft inside.

◆ *4 to 6 servings*

Spinach Omelet

Tortilla de Espinacas ◆ *Colombia*

2 tablespoons olive oil

3 potatoes, peeled and sliced

1 onion, chopped

1 red chili pepper, chopped

1 bunch fresh spinach, coarsely
  chopped

6 eggs

Salt and pepper

Pinch of chives

In a skillet, fry the potatoes in 1 tablespoon of the oil for about 15 minutes. Add the onion and chili pepper and fry for a few more minutes. Add the spinach and fry for 3 minutes. Set aside. Beat the eggs and add salt and pepper to taste. Heat the remaining tablespoon of olive oil and add in eggs. Cook over low heat until it starts to set on the bottom. Then add the potato and spinach mixture on top. Cook for about 10 minutes, then slide the *tortilla* onto a serving dish and cut into wedges. Sprinkle chives over the omelet before serving.

◆ *4 to 6 servings*

Avocados in Bed

PALTA EN CAMA ◆ *Argentina*

Handful of green lettuce leaves
2 ripe avocados, peeled, pitted, and
   finely chopped
1 small tomato, chopped
2 green onions, chopped
½ jalapeño pepper, chopped
2 hard-boiled eggs, chopped
2 tablespoons chopped fresh
   parsley

2 tablespoons chopped red roasted
   bell pepper
1 tablespoon olive oil
1 tablespoon fresh lemon or lime
   juice
Dash of salt and pepper

Wash and dry the lettuce leaves and arrange on a nice dish. Mix the avocados, tomato, onions, jalapeño, eggs, parsley, and roasted pepper. Drizzle on the olive oil and lemon juice and add the salt and pepper. Mix well. Arrange mixture on top of lettuce leaves and refrigerate until serving.

◆ *4 to 6 servings*

Widow Potatoes

Patatas Guisadas Viudas ◆ *Spain*

6 tablespoons olive oil

1 large onion, chopped

3 pounds red potatoes, peeled and
    cut into medium chunks

1 tablespoon paprika

6 cups water

4 cubes bouillon (beef or chicken)

Few threads of saffron

2 tablespoons chopped fresh
    parsley

In a large pan, heat olive oil over medium heat. Sauté onion until golden, 5 to 6 minutes. Add potatoes. Fry, stirring, for 5 minutes and add paprika. Fry another 2 minutes, stirring occasionally. Cover with 6 cups of water and add bouillon cubes, making sure they dissolve. In a garlic press, press the saffron and half of the parsley, adding a little water. Add to the potatoes and stir, mixing well. Simmer 30 minutes until the potatoes are tender. Sprinkle with the rest of the parsley before serving.

◆ *4 to 6 servings*

Ana's Stuffed Potatoes

Papas Rellenas ◆ *Peru*

Potatoes, *papas*, or *patatas*, the food of the Inca, are one of the main ingredients in Peruvian cooking.   —Ana

6 large Idaho potatoes

1 cup cooked ground beef,
   well seasoned

1 egg, beaten

Salt and pepper

1 cup shredded Cheddar cheese

Preheat oven to 350°F. Wash and pierce the potatoes. Bake for about 30 minutes or until tender. Cut the potatoes in half, scoop the insides out, and place in a bowl, reserving skins. Mash well. Add the ground beef and the egg. Add salt and pepper to taste. Fill the potato shells with the mixture. Top with Cheddar cheese. Bake for 10 more minutes. Cool slightly before serving.

◆ *4 to 6 servings*

Nohemi's Potatoes

Patatas a la Rioja ◆ *Spain*

By far my favorite Spanish meat, *chorizo* is a spicy sausage perfect for sandwiches and a variety of other recipes. For years when anyone in my family traveled to Spain she would return with shrink-wrapped *chorizo* stowed in her suitcase. The best *chorizo* comes from Mamá's hometown, Leon. Luckily, I was able to find some *chorizo* here in America in a gourmet shop outside of Washington, D.C., and it can be ordered on the Internet as well.   —Noemi

½ cup olive oil

2 pounds potatoes, peeled and
    sliced

5 ounces *chorizo*, sliced

1 pound onions, chopped

1 pound tomatoes, peeled and
    chopped

3 red bell peppers, seeded
    and chopped

Salt and pepper

4 cups chicken stock

Heat oil in a large flameproof casserole. When hot, reduce the heat and sauté the potatoes, *chorizo*, and onions for 10 to 15 minutes. Add tomatoes and peppers. Cook 5 minutes, season with salt and pepper to taste, and add the chicken stock. Cover and simmer for 15 minutes. Serve hot.

◆ *4 to 6 servings*

Potato Gnocchi

Noquis de Papa • *Argentina*

3 large Idaho or russet potatoes

1 teaspoon salt

Dash of pepper

1 egg, beaten

$1\frac{1}{2}$ cups unbleached flour, sifted

1 can ($14\frac{1}{2}$ ounces) tomato sauce

4 tablespoons butter

Fresh grated Parmesan cheese

In a large saucepan, boil potatoes in salted water until tender. Drain and cool. Peel potatoes and pass them through a ricer or push them through a coarse sieve. Spread potatoes out on a large plate and let cool completely. On a cool working surface, gather the cold potatoes into a mound and form a hole in the center. Stir the salt and pepper into the egg and pour the mixture into the hole. Using both hands, work the eggs into the potatoes, gradually adding the flour and scraping the dough up from the surface as necessary. Work the dough just until all the ingredients are blended, 4 to 5 minutes. Lightly dust the dough, your hands, and the work surface with flour and cut the dough into 3 pieces. To shape the gnocchi, using both hands, roll each piece of dough into a $\frac{1}{2}$-inch-diameter rope. Then cut the rope at $\frac{1}{2}$-inch intervals. Bring a large pot of salted water to a rolling boil. Drop the pieces of dough into the water. As soon they come to the surface of the water, they are done. Drain in a colander and pour some cold water on the gnocchi. Reserve. In a saucepan, heat the tomato sauce. In another pan, melt the butter and sauté the gnocchi until they are warm. Pour the heated tomato sauce on top and mix well. Sprinkle with Parmesan cheese before serving.

• 4 to 6 servings

Castillian Potatoes

Patatas Castellanas ◆ *Spain*

This recipe is typical of the Castillian region, where I was born. Some of the bars in Leon offer this as *tapas* with drinks.   —Nohemi

¼ cup oil

1 onion, chopped

1 garlic clove, chopped

4½ pounds potatoes, peeled and
   cut into small chunks

1 teaspoon paprika

1 tablespoon flour

Salt and pepper

1 bay leaf

Heat oil in a saucepan and sauté onion and garlic until golden. Add potatoes and paprika and cook for a bit. Add flour and stir until potatoes are slightly brown. Add hot water just to cover. Add salt and pepper to taste, and the bay leaf. Cook slowly for 30 minutes.

◆ *4 to 6 servings*

Fried Yucca

Yuca Frita ◆ *Colombia*

1 pound yucca	1 tablespoon oil
2 cubes chicken bouillon	2 tablespoons butter

Peel and wash yucca thoroughly. Cut into 3-inch rounds. Heat enough water to cover yucca and bouillon cubes in a large pot. Gently place yucca in boiling water and cook until tender, about 20 minutes. Drain and place pieces on end and cut into 6 sections each. Fry on all sides in melted butter and oil until golden brown. Serve immediately.

◆ *4 to 6 servings*

Swiss Chard in Cream

ACELGAS EN CREMA ◆ *Argentina*

Swiss chard is a vegetable that has green leaves and belongs to the beet family. You can use Swiss chard to replace spinach in other recipes. You can also use collard greens or kale in this recipe instead of Swiss chard.   —Lilly

3 tablespoons butter	2 pounds Swiss chard
1 medium onion, chopped	Salt and pepper
1 celery stalk, chopped	½ cup half-and-half
1 jalapeño pepper, chopped	½ cup shredded Swiss cheese

Heat butter in a saucepan and sauté onion, celery, and jalapeño. Wash and drain the Swiss chard and cut white and green parts into strips. Add to saucepan, stir to mix, and season with salt and pepper to taste. Cover and simmer over low heat until the chard is tender, about 10 minutes. Stir in half-and-half. Add Swiss cheese and cook until cheese is bubbly.

◆ *4 to 6 servings*

Yucca Fritters

Yuca Frita ◆ *Colombia*

2 pounds yucca

3 garlic cloves, chopped

¼ cup chopped onions

2 to 3 eggs

1 tablespoon cornstarch

1 teaspoon baking powder

Salt and pepper

Hot sauce

Vegetable oil

Peel yucca and cut into small pieces. Process yucca pieces in a food processor until it becomes a coarse paste. Add garlic, onions, eggs, cornstarch, baking powder, and salt, pepper, and hot sauce to taste, and process again. Heat enough oil to cover the fritters in a skillet. Using 2 tablespoons of the paste at a time, place a fritter in hot oil for about 3 to 4 minutes or until brown. Drain the yucca fritters on a paper towel before serving.

◆ *4 to 6 servings*

Boiled Eggs au Gratin

Huevos Duros Gratinados ◆ *Spain*

9 hard-boiled eggs

8 ounces mushrooms, sliced

4 tablespoons butter

4 tablespoons olive oil

2 medium onions, chopped

2 tablespoons flour

2 cups milk

Salt

Dash of nutmeg

3 tablespoons dried bread crumbs

5 tablespoons butter, cut into pats

Peel the eggs and cut lengthwise. Scoop out yolks, mash well, and reserve. Place egg whites in a buttered ovenproof dish. Heat 2 tablespoons of the butter in a saucepan over medium heat. Cook mushrooms over low heat, covered, for 10 minutes. Heat 2 tablespoons of the oil and sauté onion for 8 minutes. Heat the remaining 2 tablespoons each of butter and oil in a saucepan. Add flour little by little, then milk, and salt to taste, stirring constantly. Bring to a boil and simmer for 10 minutes. Into a bowl, pour about 3 tablespoons of the sauce and mix with the mashed egg yolks, onion, mushrooms, and nutmeg. Fill egg white halves with the mix. Pour the remaining sauce over. If the sauce is too thick, add a little milk to a desired consistency. Sprinkle bread crumbs on top and dot with the pats of butter. Broil in an oven for about 5 minutes or until golden on top.

◆ *4 to 6 servings*

Brussels Sprouts with Almonds

Repollito de Bruselas con Almendras ◆ *Argentina*

¼ cup sliced almonds

1 tablespoon butter

1 package (16 ounces) frozen
    brussels sprouts

½ cup chicken broth

1 cup light cream

1 can (4 ounces) red pimientos,
    drained and chopped

1 tablespoon chopped fresh parsley

1 garlic clove, chopped

1 tablespoon fresh grated
    Parmesan cheese

Salt and pepper

In a skillet sauté almonds in butter until lightly browned. Set aside. In a saucepan cook the brussels sprouts according to package directions, adding the chicken broth to the water. In another saucepan, combine cream, pimientos, parsley, garlic, and cheese. Add salt and pepper to taste. Cook until heated through. Drain sprouts. Top with cream sauce and stir gently. Sprinkle the almonds on top before serving.

◆ *4 to 6 servings*

Pastas

LILLY

The most experienced cook in the group, Lilly began cooking when she was ten years old in her native town of Campana, Argentina. In fact, Lilly met her American husband over food. She was working as a chef's assistant in a hotel in Argentina, and her future husband was staying at the hotel on business. He came down to the restaurant one afternoon, hungry, and Lilly fixed him a sandwich. It was love at first sight! When she arrived in America, the first thing Lilly did was throw out all the frozen food from her new husband's refrigerator and she promptly began to make all the recipes she had been used to eating in Argentina—steak, roast, lamb, lots of potatoes and vegetables, pastas and fresh fruits. Lilly has always been in charge when it comes to assigning the various dishes brought by the friends to each get-together. Her expert cooking has always raised the bar for the other ladies. I remember visiting Lilly's house on beautiful Guilford Lake when I was young. They had a fantastic A-framed house and Lilly made wonderful food for the gatherings. There is nothing like good food by a lake!

—Noemi

Just a few steps from beautiful Gilford Lake, Ohio, is where I live with my husband, Rudy. We share our home with an old Siamese cat. I have lived in this area since I came to America, some twenty-three years ago. I have adapted completely to living in the U.S., indulging in canoeing, walking, and swimming at our wonderful lake. In the summertime, we live as much outside as inside. For the past sixteen years, I have combined my homemaking duties with a practice in electrolysis. My two biggest passions are cooking and gardening.

The center of my culinary style is meat, especially lamb and beef, which is not surprising since I come from Argentina, a country best known for its excellent meat. I really mastered the art of fine cooking when I was young and worked for ten years assisting various chefs in a first-class hotel. Because of the high Italian emigration in the late nineteenth century to Argentina, Italian food has made a big mark in the local cuisine and we Argentineans love pasta as much as they do in Italy.

When it comes to having get-togethers with family and friends, I enjoy smaller groups for entertaining. It's a more casual and easygoing atmosphere. My backyard has an extended porch and picnic area, ideal for outdoor gatherings. We hold a lot of parties in the summertime. I use recipes like a painter uses a brush. I start with the basic recipe idea and add different ingredients of my own. I do a lot of cooking by trial and error and I am constantly

trying new recipes. I have been interested in cooking practically all my life. I grew up watching my mother in the kitchen. Everything made was from scratch on an old kerosene stove. She was a very skillful cook and an extremely good baker. I am a firm believer that home-style cooking is a way of cooking that turns everyday ingredients into downright good food. Tasteful, but simple. That is the kind of cooking I enjoy.   —Lilly

Lilly enjoying a gathering with friends

Stuffed Manicotti

CANELONES A LA ROSSINI ◆ *Argentina*

Sundays are "pasta day" in Argentina. This is an old tradition that the Italians passed on to Argentina. Preparing fresh pasta starts early in the morning. First my sisters and I would visit the chicken coop in the backyard and collect fresh brown eggs. We started the dough with flour and olive oil. Then we rolled the dough into thin sheets and hung it on the back of chairs to dry. By then it was time to go to church, so the cutting of the dough was done later. Everything was done by hand and everyone pitched in to help. Buenos Aires, the capital city of Argentina, has several excellent pasta restaurants and the most popular pasta dishes are *Canelones a la Rossini* and *Ravioli a la Bolognesa.* —Lilly

Crepes

3 eggs

1 cup water

1 cup flour

Salt

Filling

1 pound (16 ounces) small curd
  cottage cheese

1 cup spinach, chopped and sautéed

1 tablespoon onion, chopped
  and sautéed

1 tablespoon chopped fresh parsley

1 egg

2 tablespoons fresh grated
  Parmesan cheese

Salt and pepper

Assembly

1 cup tomato sauce

Fresh grated Parmesan cheese

To make the crepes, place eggs in a blender. Add water, flour, and salt. Blend until it is a smooth batter. Place 2 tablespoons of batter in a heated crepe or omelet pan that has been oiled. Cook on each side until golden and blistery. Cover the crepes with wax paper while making sauce.

To make the filling, drain cottage cheese and mix with spinach, onion, parsley, and egg. Add Parmesan cheese, and salt and pepper to taste.

To assemble the dish, preheat oven to 350°F. Lay out the crepes on a clean surface. Place 2 tablespoons of filling in each crepe. Roll and place in oiled baking dish, seams side down. Spoon the tomato sauce on top along with the grated Parmesan cheese. Bake for 15 minutes or until hot and bubbly.

◆ *4 to 6 servings*

Spaghetti with Garlic

SPAGHETTI CON SALSA DE AJOS • *Argentina*

1 pound spaghetti

½ cup butter

½ cup olive oil

5 garlic cloves, minced

2 tablespoons chopped
fresh parsley

1 tablespoon chopped fresh basil

1 tablespoon chopped walnuts

Salt and pepper

Dash of oregano

1 cup fresh grated Romano cheese

Cook spaghetti according to the directions on the box. Drain well. Melt butter in a heavy skillet. Add oil and heat. Sauté garlic until slightly browned. Stir in parsley, basil, and walnuts. Add salt and pepper to taste, and oregano. Mix well. Add the spaghetti to the skillet and blend with the garlic sauce, mixing well. Sprinkle the Romano cheese on top before serving.

• *4 to 6 servings*

Spaghetti with Clam Sauce

SPAGHETTI A LA VONGOLE ◆ *Argentina*

½ cup butter

¼ cup olive oil

3 garlic cloves, minced

2 cans (16 ounces) minced clams, drained

¼ cup finely chopped fresh parsley

¼ teaspoon dried oregano

¼ teaspoon dried basil

Salt and pepper

1 pound spaghetti

Fresh grated Parmesan cheese

Melt butter in saucepan. Add oil and heat. Sauté garlic and clams in hot oil mixture. Stir in parsley, oregano, and basil, and salt and pepper to taste. Simmer for 10 minutes. Cook spaghetti according to the directions on the box. Drain well. Return to pot. Add sauce and toss lightly. Serve with grated Parmesan cheese.

◆ *4 to 6 servings*

Spaghetti with Red Wine Sauce

SPAGHETTI AL VINO ROJO ◆ *Argentina*

1 pound spaghetti

2 pounds sirloin, sliced into strips

Vegetable oil

¾ cup diced onions

1 cup diced green bell peppers

½ jalapeño or chili pepper, diced

2 cups peeled and diced tomatoes

½ cup red wine

2 cups beef stock

½ cup chopped celery2 tablespoons
   finely diced carrots

1 cup sliced mushrooms

Salt and pepper

2 teaspoons dried basil

1 teaspoon dried oregano

Fresh grated Romano cheese

2 teaspoons chopped fresh parsley

Cook spaghetti according to the directions on the box. Drain well. In a skillet, sauté the sirloin in a little oil. Add onions, both peppers, and tomatoes. Cook for about 5 minutes at medium heat. Add wine and stock. Simmer for 2 minutes. Add celery, carrots, mushrooms, and salt and pepper to taste. Add the basil and oregano. Simmer for 30 minutes at very low heat. Smother the spaghetti with the sauce and sprinkle with Romano cheese and parsley before serving.

◆ *4 to 6 servings*

Ziti with Bacon

ZITI CON PANCETA • *Argentina*

½ pound bacon, diced

1 onion, chopped

1 green bell pepper, seeded
and chopped

1 roasted pepper, seeded
and chopped

1 cup chopped mushrooms

½ cup half-and-half

1 pound ziti

¼ cup fresh grated Parmesan
cheese

Cook bacon until crispy in a heavy skillet. Remove bacon and drain off drippings, returning 2 tablespoons of the drippings to the skillet. Sauté onions in bacon drippings until just translucent. Add both of the peppers and the mushrooms. Cook for another 7 minutes at low heat. Add half-and-half. Mix well. Simmer at very low heat for 2 minutes. Remove from heat. Cook ziti according to the directions on the box. Drain well. Return bacon sauce to low heat, just long enough to reheat. Mix ziti with bacon sauce and bacon in a pot. Blend everything well. Add cheese and toss lightly.

• 4 to 6 servings

Penne with Mushrooms

Penne con Hongos • *Argentina*

1 pound penne pasta	2 teaspoons chopped fresh parsley
½ cup butter	Salt and pepper
¼ cup olive oil	½ cup cream
1 pound fresh mushrooms, sliced	Fresh grated Parmesan cheese

Cook penne according to the directions on the box. Drain well. Melt butter in a skillet. Add olive oil and heat. Sauté mushrooms in the hot oil. Stir in parsley. Add salt and pepper to taste. Cook for 7 minutes, stirring from time to time. Remove from heat. Add mushroom sauce to pasta, tossing lightly. Add cream and Parmesan cheese and blend well before serving.

• *4 to 6 servings*

Lilly's Lasagna

LASAGNA AL HORNO   ♦   *Argentina*

3 tablespoons butter

1 onion, finely chopped

1 cup sliced fresh mushrooms

¼ pound ham, cut into strips

1 pound fresh spinach
    or 1 bag (16 ounces) thawed
    frozen spinach, chopped

3 cups tomato sauce

10 ounces lasagna noodles

1 cup ricotta cheese

1 cup shredded mozzarella cheese

1 cup fresh grated Parmesan
    cheese

½ cup cream

Melt butter in a skillet. Sauté onion, mushrooms, and ham. Wash and dry spinach before chopping. If using frozen, drain it well. Add spinach to the skillet with the onion mixture. Add tomato sauce. Simmer uncovered for 10 minutes. Cook lasagna noodles according to the directions on the box. Drain well. Preheat the oven to 350°F. Layer half the lasagna noodles in a buttered baking dish. Spread half the sauce over the noodles. Spread half of the ricotta and mozzarella cheeses over all. Repeat the layers. Bake for about 30 minutes. Add the Parmesan cheese and the cream before serving.

♦ *4 to 6 servings*

Buenos Aires Ravioli

RAVIOLES DEL BUEN AIRE ◆ *Argentina*

Pasta Dough

3¼ cups flour

¼ teaspoon salt

3 eggs, slightly beaten

1½ cups butter, softened

½ cup lukewarm water

Filling

1 cup cooked ground chicken

1 cup cooked spinach, chopped and
    well drained

2 eggs, slightly beaten

½ cup bread crumbs

½ cup fresh grated Parmesan
    cheese

2 teaspoons chopped fresh parsley

2 garlic cloves, minced

Salt and pepper

1 teaspoon dried oregano

Assembly

2 cups tomato sauce

To make the pasta dough, sift together the flour and salt in a large bowl.
Add eggs, butter, and water. Mix until dough can be gathered into a ball.
Place dough on lightly floured surface. Knead until smooth and elastic.
Cover and let stand for 15 minutes.

To make the filling, combine chicken, spinach, eggs, bread crumbs, Parmesan cheese, parsley, garlic, salt and pepper to taste, and the oregano. Mix well.

To assemble the ravioli, divide dough in half, roll each half out to ⅛-inch thickness. Place a teaspoon of the filling at 1½-inch intervals on one sheet of dough. Cover with the second sheet of dough. Cut into squares or rounds with a knife or cookie cutter. Moisten edges and seal with a fork. Allow to dry 1 hour. Cook in boiling salted water in batches, for about 5 minutes or until ravioli are tender. Heat tomato sauce in a pan and pour over the ravioli before serving.

◆ *4 to 6 servings*

Gnocchi with Ricotta

NOQUIS DE PAPA Y RICCOTA ◆ *Argentina*

These gnocchi can be served with any good mushroom sauce.—Lilly

1 pound potatoes	¼ cup shredded Cheddar cheese
½ pound ricotta cheese	2 eggs, beaten
1 cup fresh grated Romano cheese	1½ cups flour

Peel and steam potatoes until tender. Press potatoes through a ricer or food mill. Blend the three cheeses together. Blend potatoes, cheeses, and eggs together. Add the flour slowly. Knead, creating a soft dough. Mold the dough into teaspoon-size dumplings. Place on a floured surface and press with a fork. Drop dumplings into salted, boiling water. Cook for 3 minutes or until they start to come to the surface.

◆ *4 to 6 servings*

Lamb

ANA

Peruvian cuisine has been influenced by Spanish con-quistadors, the Inca, and immigrants from Italy, China, Japan, and Africa. Born and raised in Huaraz, Peru, Ana followed her American Peace Corps husband, Tom, to the United States twenty-eight years ago. They met at a dance, dated for two-and-a-half years, and were married in Peru. They have a daughter, Diana, and a son, Brian. At first Ana began cooking American foods, taught to her by her new American family, but soon she began to experiment with the foods she had eaten in Peru—salted beef *(lomo saltado)*, French fries, beef cubes, onions, rice, and garlic. In Peru, gar-lic and onion are the main seasonings and Ana has learned how to include these in a variety of her recipes.   —Noemi

Like in most South American countries, lunch is the largest meal of the day. Generally one eats soup and a rice plate or potatoes with a variety of meat dishes. Some families serve salad as a main dish dressed with oil, lemon juice, salt, and pepper. Peruvian food is generally seasoned with cumin and pepper, which give it its rich flavor.

My large family consists of three brothers and three sisters—two of my sisters are magnificent cooks. What I most remember about the food I ate growing up was never knowing what wonderful dishes would be served. As I came in the door each day, I could smell the garlic and onions and my imagination and stomach ran wild wondering what we would be eating. I loved the anticipation of not knowing what we might have to eat each day.

In the twenty-eight years that I have lived in Ohio, I have always celebrated Christmas Eve. This is very important in Peru. After attending Mass at midnight, Peruvians run home to wrap their gifts. I still do this every Christmas with my family.

For many years, Nohemi, Lilly, Nora, and I have celebrated New Year's Eve together. We each bring the customs of our countries to the celebration. I give presents that are yellow. Nora, from Colombia, makes each of us run down the driveway with a suitcase for good luck and happy travels. Nohemi, from Spain, has us each eat twelve grapes for good wishes. We always eat a meal of pork and sauerkraut.   —Ana

Ana (second from left) toasts to the New Year with Nora (left), Nohemi (third from left), and Lilly (right)

Leg of Lamb

Pierna de Cordero ◆ *Peru*

This dish may be served with sweet potatoes.   —Ana

1 leg of lamb (about 6 to 8 pounds)
2 garlic cloves, cut into slivers
1 can (16 ounces) tomatoes,
   drained
½ cup red wine
1 tablespoon chopped fresh parsley

1 teaspoon salt
½ teaspoon dried rosemary,
   crushed
⅛ teaspoon pepper
½ cup chicken stock or water

Preheat oven to 350°F. Cut small slits in lamb and insert the slivers of garlic into the cuts. Combine remaining ingredients except the stock or water. Pour over meat. Place meat in a roasting pan and roast for 10 minutes. Pour chicken stock or water into the pan. Baste the lamb with the broth or water every 10 minutes. Keep roasting and basting the lamb for 2 hours or until very tender.

◆ *4 to 6 servings*

Lamb Chilindron

CORDERO EN CHILINDRÓN ◆ *Spain*

4 tablespoons olive oil

1 onion, chopped

3 garlic cloves, chopped

1 sprig of parsley

4 tomatoes, peeled and chopped

12 lamb rib chops

6 roasted red peppers,
  cut into strips

Salt and pepper

2 tablespoons chopped fresh
  parsley

Heat 2 tablespoons of the oil and add onion, 1 of the chopped garlic cloves, and the parsley sprig. Cook slowly for 5 minutes. Stir in tomatoes and cook 10 minutes longer. Heat the remaining 2 tablespoons of oil in a casserole and add lamb chops. Brown chops and add the remaining 2 chopped garlic cloves, the vegetables from the frying pan, and the red peppers. Season with salt and pepper to taste. Cover and cook slowly 1 hour. Sprinkle parsley on top before serving.

◆ *4 to 6 servings*

Peruvian Lamb Stew

GUISO DE CORDERO A LA PERUANA ◆ *Peru*

This stew should be served hot, with plenty of French bread. —Ana

2 tablespoons olive oil

2 pounds boneless lean lamb,
  cut into 1-inch cubes

1 large onion, chopped

1 green bell pepper, seeded
  and chopped

½ chili pepper, chopped

1 can (8 ounces) tomato sauce

1 cup red wine

2 small zucchini, cubed

2 potatoes, cubed

2 carrots, peeled and sliced

1 green apple, cored and cubed

½ cup dried apricots, soaked in
  water for 20 minutes

Salt and pepper

Dash of oregano

Heat oil in a large skillet. Brown lamb in oil over medium heat. Add onions, both peppers, and tomato sauce, stirring constantly about 1 minute. Add wine, zucchini, potatoes, and carrots. Mix well. Cook for 15 minutes. Add more liquid if necessary. Add apple. Drain apricots and add to the stew. Season with salt and pepper to taste. Add the oregano. Simmer at low heat for 45 minutes.

◆ *4 to 6 servings*

Lamb Chops with Broiled Red Peppers

CHULETAS DE CORDERO CON PIMIENTOS ASADOS • *Spain*

There is a restaurant outside of Madrid called *El Churrascón* that has a big, beautiful patio. In the summertime, they only serve grilled lamb chops with roasted peppers and salad. They are absolutely scrumptious. There is always a long line of people waiting to be seated. In my early twenties, when I was living in Madrid, this restaurant was one of my favorite hangouts.   —Nohemi

4 red bell peppers, seeded
    and cut into strips
3 tablespoons olive oil

12 lamb chops
Salt and pepper
Paprika

Char peppers on a broiler until blackened. Let stand 15 minutes and then peel. Set peppers in a pan with 2 tablespoons of the olive oil. Preheat broiler. Rub lamb chops with salt, pepper, and paprika, and the remaining tablespoon oil. Broil for about 3 minutes on each side or until chops are done to your taste. Bring red peppers to a simmer and spoon over the lamb before serving.

◆ *6 to 8 servings*

◆

Nohemi's Birthday Fiesta

APPETIZER

Squid with Red Wine Sauce 4
Calamares con Salsa de Vino

SALAD

Rice Salad 47
Ensalada Fría de Arroz

MAIN

Lamb Chops with Broiled
Red Peppers 126
*Chuletas de Cordero con Pimientos
Asados*

DESSERT

Caramel Custard Cake 262
Flan

WINE

Any good red wine

◆ ◆ ◆

Lamb Chops with Lemon Sauce

CHULETAS DE CORDERO CON SALSA DE LIMÓN ◆ *Peru*

2 tablespoons olive oil

6 shoulder lamb chops, each
    about 1 inch thick

1 garlic clove, minced

1 tablespoon dried parsley flakes

½ cup dry white wine

½ cup water

2 tablespoons fresh lemon juice

3 egg yolks, slightly beaten

Heat oil in a skillet. Brown chops well in hot oil. Add garlic, parsley, wine, and water. Cook over medium heat, about 15 minutes or until chops are tender. Remove chops and keep warm. Cook liquid until reduced by half. Add lemon juice to the eggs. Stir a small amount of the cooked liquid into the eggs, then pour all into skillet. Cook over low heat, stirring constantly until slightly thickened. Pour over lamb chops before serving.

◆ *4 to 6 servings*

Pork

Pork with Chili Sauce

Cerdo con Salsa de Chili ◆ *Peru*

Serve this dish with white rice and garlic bread.   —Ana

2 tablespoons olive oil

1 medium onion, chopped

1 garlic clove, minced

2 tablespoons chili powder

1½ pounds lean pork, cut into
   1½-inch cubes

2 cups canned tomatoes, broken up
   with a fork

½ teaspoon salt

½ teaspoon dried oregano

½ teaspoon cumin

⅛ teaspoon cloves

1 small cinnamon stick

Heat olive oil. Add onions and garlic. Brown slightly. Add chili powder. Stir well. Push vegetables to the sides of the pan. Brown pork on all sides. Add tomatoes, salt, oregano, cumin, cloves, and cinnamon stick. Stir well. Bring to a boil. Reduce heat to low. Cover and cook for 2 hours or until pork is very tender. Stir mixture occasionally while cooking.

◆ *4 to 6 servings*

Pork Loin in Milk

Lomo de Cerdo ◆ *Argentina*

This dish may be served with mashed potatoes. —Lilly

2 pounds boneless pork loin,
    tied up with string

4 cups milk

½ cup fresh lemon juice

Salt and pepper

2 tablespoons butter

Put pork in a flameproof dish that is just large enough to hold it snugly. Mix milk with lemon juice and pour over pork. Cover dish and refrigerate 8 to 12 hours. When ready to cook, lift pork out of milk mixture and pat dry. Season with salt and pepper. Preheat oven to 325°F. Heat butter in a skillet and brown pork all over. Put pork back into the dish with the milk together with the drippings and bake, uncovered, for 1 to 2 hours or until pork is tender. Lift pork out onto a warmed serving dish and remove the strings. Skim the fat from the sauce and pour the sauce into a pan. Reduce it over low heat until you have around 1½ cups. Pour sauce into a gravy boat and serve separately. Slice meat before serving.

◆ *4 to 6 servings*

NOHEMI

Nohemi (center) with son Kris and daughter Raquel

A native of León, Spain, Nohemi distinctly recalls the first time, twenty-four years ago, she went to a grocery store in the United States and how different it was. In Spain, food is sold in open markets, and fillets of steak, pork, and fish are cut fresh to your specifications. Rice, beans, peas, and other foods are sold in bulk. Instead, in America Nohemi found pre-packaged foods. She couldn't read or speak English and it was difficult to shop without seeing what was inside the packages. Nohemi tried to cook the recipes she recalled from Spain—fried eggs, *tortillas* (an omelet-like dish usually made with eggs and potatoes), meats, and chicken with rice. Slowly, she also began to include foods in her repertoire that defined Spanish cooking for her—lentils, garbanzo beans (chickpeas), fish, and a lot of fruits and vegetables. Today, she has successfully incorporated these foods and many others in a wealth of recipes that she has adapted and changed over the years. When Spanish recipes called for ingredients like *chorizo* or *morcilla* (both types of Spanish sausages) unavailable in the U.S. until recently, Nohemi learned to do without those foods or substituted ingredients found here. Some recipes required seafood not found in small towns, and Nohemi substituted with what she found locally.   —Noemi

I met my American husband, Ray, in a hotel in Madrid, where he was traveling on business. We share three children—Noemi, Kris, and Raquel; two children from my husband's previous marriage—Bruce and Robin; three granddaughters—Brooke, Alexandra, and Ashtyn; one grandson Robert; and one grandchild expected in June 2003. We live on a farm in western Pennsylvania. Although I have a degree in social work, I work part-time in retail in a store close to my home. Whenever possible I accompany my husband on trips related to work, especially now that our children are grown and live on their own.

Good nutrition has always been a very important factor in making recipes for my family. Since I was raised on a Mediterranean diet, my cooking has always been done from scratch with an emphasis in fresh fruits and vegetables for a well-balanced meal. A mixture of Spanish and American cooking has prevailed during holiday meals. During Christmas, American cooking has gone hand in hand with the traditional *Roscón de Reyes* (Christmas Cake on page 227) celebrated on January 6th. Gatherings like July 4th with friends and family boasted hot dogs, hamburgers, Colombian and Peruvian rice salads, delicious Argentinean liquored cakes, and Spanish *Flan* (Caramel Custard Cake on page 262). The eating of twelve grapes at the turn of the

New Year has been a must in my home. I still have eight siblings and many cousins and aunts in Spain. When I go back home to visit, they all make sure to cook traditional childhood dishes for my enjoyment. I am sure to pick up additional tips and recipes to bring back to America and incorporate in my daily cooking. My favorite foods are fresh fish, seafood typically found in northern Spain, and dishes that my children aren't too crazy about, like tripe, tongue, and squid.

Most Spanish recipes have onions, garlic, peppers, and parsley. Most Americans have the misconception that Spanish food is spicy hot. That is not true. We use paprika, which is sweet not hot. Olive oil is the main oil used for cooking, with peanut and sunflower oils coming close behind. We also typically use white or red cooking wine in our recipes. The alcohol evaporates with the cooking, leaving behind a distinctive "Spanish" flavor to dishes.

The *chicas* and I have been friends for over two decades. Although we all share many things in common, we are also unique individuals. Ana is the calm and patient one of the group. She speaks softly and doesn't get rattled easily. She is always involved in volunteer work at the school where she teaches Spanish and out in the community. Ana always has beautiful flowers in her yard. We have been friends for almost twenty-five years and she is always loyal and generous. Lilly is the cook of the group. Not only is she a good cook, she loves to do it. She is the one who organizes the meals for our gatherings. She has a dry sense of humor and loves to take care of her garden and flowers. A cancer survivor, Lilly has a strength that I absolutely admire. Nora is the youngest in the group by one year. Small and always in a flurry of movement, she only sits when we gather to talk and be together. She is a money saver and has taught the rest of us the importance of saving our pennies. Like me, she does not have a green thumb, and it seems that flowers and vegetables wilt in her presence.   —Nohemi

Orange Pork Loin

Lomo a la Naranja ◆ *Spain*

2 pounds pork loin roast

¼ cup olive oil

1 onion, cut into rings

1 large carrot, julienned

1 teaspoon arrowroot

2 tablespoons sherry

2 oranges, zested, then peeled,
    segmented, and chopped

In a large pan, brown the roast in the oil over medium high heat. Add onion and carrot. Cover and cook slowly for about 1 hour or until tender. Thinly slice the roast and keep warm. Puree remaining contents of pan in a blender and return to pan. Stir in arrowroot and sherry. Cook gently for a few minutes until creamy. Add orange zest and segments and cook for 5 minutes. Pour sauce over meat before serving.

◆ *4 to 6 servings*

Sweet Loin of Pork

Lomo de Cerdo Dulce ◆ *Argentina*

B arding a cut of meat means wrapping it in a thin slice of back fat. This keeps the meat moist as it cooks and adds flavor.   —Noemi

Pork

3 pounds boned pork loin roast,
   barded, rolled, and tied
1 tablespoon chopped fresh parsley
1 tablespoon dried oregano

1 teaspoon dried thyme
Salt and pepper
3 garlic cloves, minced

Sauce

2 tablespoons butter
1 green onion, chopped
2 tart apples, such as Granny
   Smith, peeled, cored, and
   chopped

¼ cup sugar
½ cup apple cider
Dash of cinnamon
Dash of nutmeg
Salt and pepper

To prepare the pork, preheat oven to 375°F. Untie the pork loin and set barding fat aside. Lay pork out flat. Sprinkle with parsley, oregano, thyme, and salt and pepper to taste. Add minced garlic. Reroll the loin, replace the barding fat, and tie into a nice shape. Put loin on a rack in a roasting pan and roast for about 1 to 1½ hours.

To make the sauce, melt butter in a skillet and add the green onion and apples. Cook over low heat, stirring occasionally until tender. Let apple mixture cool, then transfer it to a food processor. Add sugar, cider, cinnamon, and nutmeg. Blend until smooth. Season with salt and pepper to taste. Return sauce to pan and reheat just before serving. When pork is ready, remove from oven and let rest 10 minutes before carving. Serve with the sauce.

◆ *6 to 8 servings*

Honey Marsala Ham

Jamón con Miel y Marsala ◆ *Colombia*

1 smoked, fully cooked ham (about
    10 pounds)
1 teaspoon ground allspice
24 whole cloves
¼ cup honey

1 cup crushed pineapple
1 cup Marsala wine
Cranberry-sherry relish
    (recipe follows)

Preheat oven to 275°F. Trim excess fat from ham, leaving just a ⅛-inch-thick layer of fat. Score sides and top of ham in a diamond pattern. Sprinkle allspice over ham and place on a broiler pan coated with cooking spray. Press cloves into ham. Drizzle with honey and bake for 30 minutes. Add crushed pineapple. Baste ham all over. Add Marsala wine and keep cooking for another hour, basting every 15 minutes. Place ham on an oval dish and cover with foil. Let stand 15 minutes before carving. Serve with cranberry-sherry relish (see below).

◆ *6 to 8 servings*

Cranberry-Sherry Relish

1 medium orange	3 whole cloves
2 cups sweet sherry	½ cup sugar
1 bay leaf	1 bag (12 ounces) fresh cranberries

Remove zest from the orange using a vegetable peeler, making sure not to get any of the white part of the rind. Combine orange zest, sherry, bay leaf, and cloves in a medium pan. Bring to a simmer over medium heat. Cook for 20 minutes or until reduced to 1 cup. Strain mixture through a sieve over a bowl. Discard solids. Return mixture to pan and stir in the sugar. Add cranberries. Cook over medium heat 10 minutes or until cranberries pop, stirring occasionally. Spoon into bowl.

◆ *Makes* 3 cups relish

Glazed Ham

Jamón Glaceado ◆ *Peru*

1 boneless ham (about 5 pounds)	½ cup apple cider
2 cups Marsala wine	1 tablespoon prepared horseradish
½ cup honey	mustard

Preheat oven to 350°F. Place ham in a roasting pan. Pour wine into pan and cover. Roast in oven for about 1 hour. Baste occasionally with wine. Remove from oven. Increase temperature to 400°F. In a bowl, mix honey, cider, and mustard. Score top of ham. Spread honey mixture on top. Return to oven. Bake for 20 minutes or until glaze forms on top of ham. Remove from oven. Let ham stand 15 minutes before carving.

◆ *4 to 6 servings*

Roasted Pork with Prunes

Cerdo Horneado con Salsa de Ciruelas • *Colombia*

½ cup apple cider

½ cup pitted prunes, halved

1 tablespoon olive oil

1 pound pork tenderloin

Salt and pepper

¼ cup chopped green olives

2 tablespoons fresh lemon juice

1 teaspoon dried rosemary

2 garlic cloves, minced

⅛ teaspoon crushed red pepper

1 (14 ounce) can chicken stock

¼ cup Marsala or port wine

1 tablespoon water

1 teaspoon cornstarch

Combine apple cider and prunes in a small pan. Cover and let stand for 20 minutes or until prunes are soft. Bring to a boil and boil for 10 minutes. Remove from heat. Heat oil in a heavy skillet over medium heat until hot. Sprinkle pork with salt and pepper to taste. Add pork to skillet. Cook 5 minutes, browning on all sides. Add olives, lemon juice, rosemary, garlic, and red pepper. Add the can of chicken stock. Mix well. Bake for 30 minutes. Remove pork from skillet. Set aside and keep warm. Return prune mixture to the stove and heat until warm. Add Marsala wine. Combine water and cornstarch in a small bowl. Add cornstarch to prunes. Bring to a medium boil. Reduce heat and simmer until slightly thick. Serve sauce with the pork.

• *4 to 6 servings*

Pork Roast with Green Sauce

Cerdo Asado con Salsa Verde • *Peru*

This roast may be served with white rice.   —Ana

2 medium onions, chopped

1 green bell pepper, seeded and chopped

1 red bell pepper, seeded and chopped

½ cup chopped celery

3 carrots, peeled and sliced

1 loin or shoulder pork roast (about 5 pounds)

2 teaspoons salt

½ teaspoon dried oregano

½ teaspoon ground coriander

¾ cup sherry or port wine

Green sauce (recipe follows)

Place onions, both peppers, celery, and carrots in a roasting pan. Rub pork with salt, oregano, and coriander. Place pork on top of vegetables. Add sherry. Cover and roast for 2½ hours at 350°F. Add more sherry if necessary. Slice and serve with the green sauce (see below).

◆ *6 to 8 servings*

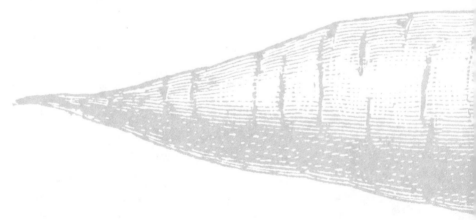

Green Sauce

3 tablespoons olive oil

1 medium onion, chopped

2 garlic cloves, peeled and chopped

1 can (10 ounces) Mexican green
   tomatoes *(tomatillos)*, drained,
   with liquid reserved

1 teaspoon dried oregano

1 tablespoon wine vinegar

Salt and pepper

Heat 1 tablespoon of the olive oil in a small skillet. Sauté onion and garlic until limp. In blender or food processor, combine tomatillos, ½ the reserved liquid from the tomatillos, onion, garlic, the remaining 2 tablespoons of olive oil, and oregano. Puree. Heat skillet once again over moderate heat. Pour in sauce. Cook for 10 minutes. Remove from heat. Add wine vinegar, and salt and pepper to taste. Chill sauce before serving.

◆ *Makes* 1 cup sauce

Lilly's Pork Chops

COSTELETAS DE CERDO NORTEÑAS ◆ *Argentina*

When I was growing up, my family's old house was complete with a chicken coop, a garden, a fruit orchard, and an old fig tree. Mother was always busy in the kitchen, especially on Sundays and holidays. I was always thrilled to help, as were my sisters, with the cooking.   —Lilly

6 pork chops, each about
  1½ inches thick

Salt

Paprika

¼ teaspoon nutmeg

12 whole cloves

2 tablespoons canola oil

½ cup dry red wine

6 slices of pineapple

3 tablespoons sugar

3 tablespoons butter

6 tart apples, peeled, cored, and
  quartered

Preheat oven to 375°F. Season the chops with salt and paprika to taste, and the nutmeg. With a knife make two cuts in each chop and insert 1 whole clove in each cut (2 cloves in each chop). Arrange chops in an oiled baking dish. Sprinkle canola oil and the wine on top. Bake for 10 minutes, then add pineapple and 2 tablespoons of the sugar. Cover and cook for another 5 minutes. Heat butter in a skillet. Add apples and the remaining tablespoon of sugar. Stir frequently, trying not to break apples. If mixture is too thick, you can add some apple cider or apple juice. Cook until apples are tender. Arrange apple mixture on top of chops and pineapple. Bake for another 15 to 20 minutes or until chops are tender.

◆ *4 to 6 servings*

Pork Chops with Fruit

CHULETAS DE CERDO CON FRUTAS ◆ *Colombia*

¾ cup pitted prunes, halved

¾ cup dried apricots, halved

¾ cup dried pears, quartered

4 pork chops

Salt and pepper

2 tablespoons olive oil

1 medium onion, chopped

1 medium green bell pepper,
 seeded and chopped

2 garlic cloves, minced

1 cup chicken stock

1 cup dry white wine

Put prunes in a bowl with apricots and pears. Pour enough water to cover fruit and let soak for 30 minutes. Season chops with salt and pepper to taste. Heat oil in a skillet and sauté chops until they are golden brown. Transfer chops to a casserole. Preheat oven to 350°F. In the same oil, sauté onion, bell pepper, and garlic until they are tender. Add to casserole. Arrange fruit over chops. Pour chicken stock and wine to cover the chops (adding more if necessary). Cover the casserole and bake for about 1 hour or until the pork is very tender.

◆ *4 servings*

Pork Chops with Rice

Chuletas de Cerdo con Arroz ◆ *Peru*

4 pork chops, each about
    1 inch thick
3 tablespoons olive oil
1 medium onion, chopped
1 green bell pepper, seeded and
    chopped

1 garlic clove, minced
1 cup long-grain rice
2 cups hot chicken stock
2 tablespoons dry sherry
1 tablespoon chopped fresh parsley
½ cup sliced almonds

Sauté pork chops in olive oil in a large heavy skillet until chops are browned. Remove from skillet. Add onion, bell pepper, and garlic to the skillet. Sauté over medium heat until soft. Add rice and cook for 5 minutes. Combine hot chicken stock and dry sherry. Pour over rice mixture. Top with pork chops. Cover and reduce heat to low. Cook for 20 to 25 minutes or until liquid is absorbed. Top chops with parsley and almonds before serving.

◆ 4 servings

Madrid-Style Tripe

Callos a la Madrileña ◆ *Spain*

To keep salt from clumping, place a few grains of rice in the bottom of the salt shaker. But aside from its use as a spice, salt has other practical purposes. Salt can be used to put out the fire in a fireplace. Mixed with vinegar, it cleans tea stains. A little salt on your fingers when handling fish prevents it from being slippery. When pressing garlic in a mortar, sprinkle a little salt to prevent slipping. —Nohemi

2 pounds tripe	¼ pound chorizo, diced
Salt	2 tablespoons tomato paste
Vinegar	2 teaspoons flour or arrowroot
2 pig feet, blanched	1 teaspoon paprika
2 tablespoons olive oil	2 chili peppers, seeded and
1 medium onion, chopped	chopped
2 garlic cloves, chopped	Salt and pepper
¼ pound cooked ham, diced	1 tablespoon chopped fresh parsley

Cut tripe into 8 × 7-inch pieces. Scrape with a knife (a brush will work well also) and rub tripe with plenty of salt and vinegar. Rinse in water several times. In a pan of water, bring tripe to a hard boil and rinse immediately (reserve liquid). When it cools down, cut tripe into strips. Put tripe and pig feet into a heavy casserole and cover with water and cook slowly for about 1½ hours. Heat oil and sauté onion and garlic for 10 minutes. Add ham, chorizo, and tomato paste and cook a few more minutes. Combine flour with reserved liquid from tripe and add. Add paprika and stir well with a wooden spoon. Pour mixture into the casserole. Add chili peppers, and salt and pepper to taste. Cook very slowly for 15 minutes until very tender. Sprinkle with parsley before serving.

◆ *4 to 6 servings*

Nora's Tripe

Mondongo en Salsa ◆ *Colombia*

This dish may be served with white rice.   —Nora

2 pounds tripe, washed and cut
    into ½-inch strips

2 ham hocks

2 tablespoons finely chopped onion

2 tablespoons finely chopped red
    bell pepper

2 tablespoons finely chopped fresh
    coriander

2 garlic cloves, chopped

2 medium tomatoes, diced

2 jalapeño or chili peppers, seeded
    and chopped

2 teaspoons salt

3 tablespoons Worcestershire
    sauce

1½ cups beef stock

Black pepper

Dried oregano

1 bay leaf

2 carrots, peeled and diced

2 potatoes, peeled and diced

Preheat oven to 350°F. Put everything except carrots and potatoes in a roasting pan. Cook for 1 to 1½ hours. Add carrots and cook for another 15 minutes. Add potatoes and cook until done. Add more beef stock if necessary. Remove bay leaf before serving.

◆ *4 to 6 servings*

Beef

◆ ANA'S BEEF SIRLOIN 167
Lomo Saltado ◆ *Peru*

◆ LILLY'S MEAT PIE 168
Pastel de Carne ◆ *Argentina*

Steak with Ham and Olives

Filetes Rellenos de Jamón y Aceitunas ◆ *Spain*

Salt and pepper

6 thin boneless sirloin steaks

6 slices baked ham

½ cup chopped green olives with
   pimiento

1½ cups olive oil

1 medium onion, chopped

1 garlic clove, chopped

3 tablespoons flour

1 cup white wine

2 cubes beef bouillon

½ teaspoon choice of dried herbs
   such as thyme, rosemary, or
   marjoram

3½ cups water

Juice of 1 lemon

Salt and pepper the steaks to taste. Place one slice of ham over each. Place small amount of olives in center over ham. Roll each steak and secure it with a toothpick or string. Heat oil in a saucepan. Fry steak rolls until golden. Reserve on a plate. In the same saucepan, remove some of the oil and sauté onion and garlic until golden, for 10 minutes. Add flour. Stir and add wine, bouillon cubes, herbs, and water, stirring constantly. Bring to a boil and add steak rolls. Simmer 1¼ hours. Add lemon juice and cook another 15 minutes. If meat is not done, let it cook a while longer. Remove toothpicks or string and place steak rolls on serving platter. Strain sauce, pressing so the onion flavor is retained. Cover steak rolls with sauce before serving.

◆ *6 servings*

A WALK DOWN MEMORY LANE

by Lilly

I met the *chicas* or "girls" twenty-something years ago. First I met Ana. She was in a beauty salon at the same time that my mother-in-law was visiting the salon. My mother-in-law picked up on Ana's Spanish accent and told her about me. The next thing I remember, we were talking on the telephone. She already knew Nora and Nohemi, so we tentatively decided to meet. Ana and Nora used to have a little craft shop in downtown Salem, Ohio, mostly selling silver jewelry and items from Peru. So I decided to play a little trick on them. I showed up one morning unannounced. There was only one of them working that day and from Ana's description I realized that Nora was the one behind the counter. Very politely, she asked me if I needed help. I said, "No I am just browsing." And she continued to work on a craft she had in front of her. I think it was some type of embroidery. After a couple of minutes, I decided to reveal myself, so I got closer to her and said in Spanish, "So you are the girl from Colombia." She was really surprised and I had my fun for the day.

What can I tell you about the girls? They are all different and unique. They are remarkable women that adapted to a new country, a different culture, a new language, but never lost their heritage and their sense of being a Latina first. Being the oldest of the group, I have watched them start as young ladies, then start families and accomplish their professional goals. If I had to define each of them, this is what I would say.

Nohemi, or "España" as I sometimes call her, is just that, a *salerosa*, a person who has a zest for life. I can't think of anybody else that represents her country any better than she does. She is a very warm person and she certainly has a very open mind. What she thinks is what you get, but you can always rely on her honesty and thoughtfulness. She has raised a wonderful family, passing on her Spanish values and native language to her children. She is very committed to our group, and although she lives in Pennsylvania (about an hour from the rest of us) she is the first to arrive to our gatherings.

Ana is the soft spoken one of the group. She has incredibly good taste. Her house represents that taste. She can turn any room into something very cozy and add her own personal touches. She has completed her college education here in America and become a very accomplished teacher. She loves gardening, like me, and her yard turns into a showcase of color and design in the summertime. Ana enjoys my cooking very much. We always tease her about how slow she eats. When everyone else is ready for dessert, she is still testing and nibbling on the main course! Like Nohemi, her children were raised in a Spanish-speaking home and her menus always include food from her native Peru.

Nora is the petite lady from Colombia. She is perky and dynamic, always moving around and doing things with a lot of energy. She has a positive outlook on life and I am convinced that there is nothing in this world that will keep her down. She went through some rough times, a divorce and becoming

a single mother, but she never complained and instead always looked ahead. She enrolled in beauty school and got her cosmetology diploma. Nora always faces life with a smile on her face and a hope for better things to come.

These are my three friends, all different and unique. Our acquaintance started over twenty years ago and has developed into a close, caring, and fun friendship of Spanish women that share special occasions together, celebrate triumphs, and overcome trials. We have been there for each other in times of sorrow and in times of joy. I admire each one of them and I am very proud to call them my friends.

The four friends enjoying a get-together From left to right: Nohemi, Lilly, Nora and Ana

Steak with Black Pepper and Mushrooms

Filetes con Pimienta y Champiñones • *Argentina*

This dish may be served with mashed potatoes.   —Lilly

2 tablespoons black peppercorns, coarsely crushed

½ teaspoon hot pepper flakes

4 boneless sirloin steaks or filets mignons, each about 2 inches thick

3 tablespoons vegetable oil

1 tablespoon butter

2 cups sliced mushrooms

½ cup red wine

½ cup cream

Combine the peppercorns and hot pepper flakes and press onto both sides of the steaks. Heat 1 tablespoon of the oil with the butter in a heavy frying pan that will be large enough to accommodate the steaks in one layer. Add mushrooms and cook over medium heat, stirring and turning them occasionally, until mushrooms are wilted, about 5 minutes. Increase the heat to medium high and continue cooking until the liquid from the mushrooms evaporates and they are lightly browned. With a slotted spoon, remove mushrooms from the pan and reserve. Add the remaining 2 tablespoons of oil to the frying pan. When it is very hot, add the steaks. Fry until browned, about 2 minutes on each side. Continue cooking to desired degree of doneness. Remove steaks from pan and keep hot. Pour off all the fat from the pan. Add the wine and bring to a boil, stirring and scraping to mix in the browned bits from the bottom of the pan. Add the cream, bring back to a boil and boil for 1 minute. Stir in the mushrooms and reheat them. Pour the sauce over the steaks before serving.

◆ *4 servings*

Onion Steak

Bistec Encebollado ◆ *Colombia*

This steak may be served with mashed potatoes.   —Nora

6 sirloin steaks, each about ¾ inch thick	Salt and pepper
½ teaspoon garlic salt	1 large onion, cut into rings
1 teaspoon Worcestershire sauce	2 tablespoons butter
	2 tablespoons olive oil

Mix steaks with garlic salt, Worcestershire sauce, and salt and pepper to taste. Set aside. In a large skillet, brown onion in butter and oil until golden. Remove onion from skillet and set on plate. Place steaks in skillet over high heat. Fry both sides to desired doneness. Place steaks on serving plate. Return onions to hot skillet with meat drippings for one minute, stirring well. Top meat with onions before serving.

◆ *4 to 6 servings*

Stuffed Rolled Flank Steak

Matambre Relleno ◆ *Argentina*

The Spanish name for this recipe translates into "kill hunger," and indeed this is a satisfying dish ideal for a picnic or Sunday brunch.   —Lilly

1 teaspoon dried oregano

1 garlic clove, minced

2 pounds flank steak

½ cup wine vinegar

6 large carrots, quartered lengthwise

1 cup slightly cooked spinach

4 hard-boiled eggs, cut into wedges

1 large onion, cut into rings

3 tablespoons chopped fresh parsley

1 teaspoon salt

1 teaspoon cayenne

1 large roasted red bell pepper, seeded and chopped

Olive oil

2 cups beef stock

Mix oregano and garlic and spread over steak. Sprinkle ½ cup of the vinegar over the steak. Cover and refrigerate overnight. Cook carrots until they are tender. Add spinach. Preheat oven to 400°F. Remove beef from marinade and pat dry with paper towels. Place beef cut side up on a flat surface with a side of each overlapping about 2 inches. With a meat mallet, pound overlapping edges together. Spread spinach over entire beef surface. Arrange cooked carrots crosswise over spinach. Place egg wedges and onion rings over carrots and spinach. Sprinkle with parsley, salt, cayenne, and red pepper. Beginning on a short side, roll beef and filling. Tie with strings at 2 to 3 inch intervals. Place in a large roasting pan. Pour some oil over top and bake uncovered about 10 minutes. Pour in stock. Cover and roast 1 hour, adding more stock as needed. At the end of the cooking time, turn off oven. Open door slightly and let the beef stand in the oven 10 minutes. Remove the strings, slice the beef, and arrange on a platter.

◆ 4 to 6 servings

Chimichurri Steak

CARNE CHIMICHURRI ◆ *Argentina*

The Argentinean spit roast barbecue or *asado criollo* originated with the *gauchos*, cowboys of the wide rolling plains of Argentina that stretch for miles. A barbecue in your backyard or on your patio is a common way to entertain family and friends. *Asados* consist of grilled sausages and various types of meat. It is an art to be a *parrillero*, or "grill master," and it takes years to master it to perfection. In Argentina men are usually in charge of the grilling. Unlike in America, meat is not basted with barbecue sauce. Instead, grilled meat is served with a semi-hot sauce called chimichurri. The recipe that follows is for meat with chimichurri sauce.   —Lilly

2 pounds short ribs

2 pounds rump or flank steak

1 pound sirloin steak

1 pound blood sausage

1 or 2 beef kidneys

1 or 2 tripe

Chimichurri sauce (recipe follows)

It takes about an hour for a fire of wood and charcoal to burn down and be ready for use. Place the meats on the grill in the above sequence so they are hot and crispy on the outside and red and juicy on the inside. When meats are done, serve with chimichurri sauce (see below).

Chimichurri Sauce

2 medium onions, finely chopped

1 green bell pepper, seeded
   and chopped

1 jalapeño pepper, seeded
   and chopped

1 garlic clove, chopped

3 tablespoons chopped fresh
   parsley

1 teaspoon dried oregano

Salt and pepper

$\frac{1}{2}$ cup olive oil

3 to 4 tablespoons red
   wine vinegar

In a bowl, combine the onions, both peppers, garlic, parsley, and oregano, mixing lightly. Season with salt and pepper to taste. In a small bowl, beat together the oil and vinegar. Pour over the vegetables and mix. Use this sauce to baste meats.

◆ *8 to 10 servings*

*The four ladies with family and
friends enjoying an outdoor barbecue*

Boiled Beef and Vegetables

Olla de Carne ◆ *Colombia*

This dish is best when made a day ahead of serving. Serve with white rice. —Nora

1 to 1½ pounds lean stewing beef

1 pound beef ribs

5 cups water

½ cup chopped green bell pepper

½ cup finely chopped onion

½ cup diced celery

3 carrots, diced

2 green plantains, cut into 4 pieces

½ pound yucca, peeled and cut into pieces

2 sweet potatoes, peeled and halved

3 potatoes, peeled and halved

1 summer squash, cut into chunks

2 ears of corn, cut in half

1 bay leaf

2 garlic cloves, peeled

2 teaspoons salt

Cut both meats into pieces and place in a pot with bell pepper, onion, celery, and carrots. Add 5 cups of water and simmer over low heat for 1 hour. Strain broth and add the rest of the vegetables including bay leaf and garlic cloves. Simmer for 1 hour or until meat is tender and vegetables are done. Add salt.

◆ *4 to 6 servings*

Lilly's Beef Stew

GUISO CRIOLLO ◆ *Argentina*

This stew may be served with garlic bread. —Lilly

Flour for dredging

Salt and pepper

1 ½ pounds boneless beef, such
    as chuck or round, cut into
    1 ½-inch cubes

3 tablespoons olive oil

2 large onions, chopped

1 green bell pepper, seeded
    and chopped

2 celery stalks, coarsely chopped

2 large carrots, peeled and
    thickly sliced

2 turnips, cubed

1 cup canned chunky tomatoes

2 cups beef stock

1 bay leaf

Dried oregano

1 cup peeled and cubed potatoes

2 green apples, cored and cubed

½ cup pitted prunes, halved

Put flour in a plastic bag and season with salt and pepper to taste. Add beef cubes, a few at a time, and toss to coat. Remove them, shaking off excess flour. Heat oil in a skillet or flameproof casserole over medium heat. Add cubes of beef in batches and brown them well on all sides. Remove them to a dish as they are browned. Add a little more oil to the casserole as needed. Add onions, bell pepper, celery, carrots, turnips, and tomatoes. Brown them all over, stirring frequently. Return beef cubes to the casserole. Add the beef stock and bay leaf. Add salt, pepper, and oregano to taste. Lower heat and add potatoes, apples, and prunes. Simmer for 1 to 1 ½ hours until beef is tender.

◆ 4 to 6 servings

Beef Stew with Dried Fruit

Guiso de Carne con Frutas Secas ◆ *Colombia*

This is one of the many beef stews with dried fruit that are very popular in many South American countries. The recipes originally come from Spain, whose food was influenced by the Moors. This stew may be served with rice.   —Nora

1 cup of dried fruit (¼ cup whole
   pitted prunes, ¼ cup whole
   dried apricots, ¼ cup dried
   peaches, halved, ¼ cup dried
   pears, halved)
1½ cups warm water
3 tablespoons olive oil
1 medium onion, chopped
1 medium green bell pepper,
   seeded and chopped

1 garlic clove, minced
½ cup chopped celery
3 pounds boneless beef, such
   as chuck or round, cut into
   1½-inch cubes
Salt and pepper
1 cup red wine

Put the dried fruits into a bowl with warm water and soak for 1 hour, turning fruits from time to time. Drain and reserve the liquid and set fruits aside. Heat oil in a skillet and sauté onion, bell pepper, garlic, and celery. Add beef and cook for 5 minutes. Season with salt and pepper to taste. Pour in wine and the reserved liquid from the fruit. Bring to a boil, reduce heat to low. Add the fruit. Cover and simmer for 30 more minutes. If the sauce is too thick, add a little more wine.

◆ *4 to 6 servings*

Braised Tongue

Lengua Estofada ◆ *Spain*

To take the odor of garlic away from your hands after cooking, rub them with a parsley sprig. —Nohemi

1 cow or calf tongue

¼ cup pork fat

4 carrots, cut into slices

2 medium onions, chopped

1 or 2 soupbones

1 cup white wine

1 bay leaf

1 teaspoon dried thyme

Dried oregano

1 garlic clove

Salt and pepper

Soak the clean tongue in cold water for 12 hours or overnight. Brush it well. Submerge tongue in a large pan of boiling water. Boil it hard for 10 minutes. Transfer pan to sink and add cold water until all the water is cold. Take the tongue out. With a sharp knife, peel off its thick skin. In a large pan, heat the pork fat. Place the drained tongue on top. Place carrots, onions, and soupbones around the tongue. Add wine, bay leaf, thyme, oregano, and garlic clove. Add salt and pepper to taste. Cover with cold water and bring to a boil. Simmer for 2 hours. Slice tongue and place over platter. Arrange some carrots around it. Discard bay leaf and pass the sauce through a blender. If it is too thin, add 1 to 2 teaspoons of flour and cook 5 more minutes. Pour sauce over tongue before serving.

◆ *4 to 6 servings*

Filet Mignon with Maitre de Hotel Butter

SOLOMILLO CON SALSA DEL MAITRE DE HOTEL ◆ *Argentina*

Meat grilled outdoors has a wonderful flavor. Searing the meat first will seal in the natural juices. If the weather is inappropriate for outdoor grilling, try broiling it in the oven for a similar effect. The bacon strips should be the same length as the circumference of the filets mignons.   —Lilly

Filets Mignons

Salt and pepper
4 filets mignons, each about 2 inches thick
4 Canadian bacon strips, each about 2 inches wide

Butter

½ cup softened butter
Juice of ½ lemon
Salt and pepper
1 tablespoon chopped fresh parsley

Assembly

4 toast rounds

To prepare the filets mignons, salt and pepper the filets to taste. Wrap Canadian bacon around each filet. Wrap a string around the filets and tie with a knot. Place the grill rack about 4 inches above the coals. Place filets on the grill and sear for 2 minutes on each side. Cook for 2 more minutes on each side for medium rare.

To make the butter, blend all the ingredients in a small bowl. Shape the mixture into small rounds and refrigerate until it is ready to use.

To assemble the dish, arrange the toast rounds on a nice dish. Put a filet on top of each toast. Arrange the butter on top of each filet before serving.

♦ *4 servings*

Beef Scallopine Marsala

Escalopes a la Marsala • *Argentina*

2 top round steaks, (each about
  $\frac{3}{4}$ pound), cut $\frac{1}{4}$ inch thick

1 egg

3 tablespoons milk

1 $\frac{1}{4}$ cups dried bread crumbs

$\frac{1}{4}$ cup fresh grated Parmesan
  cheese

1 teaspoon salt

$\frac{1}{8}$ teaspoon pepper

$\frac{1}{2}$ cup butter

1 garlic clove, sliced

$\frac{3}{4}$ cup water

2 teaspoons flour

$\frac{1}{2}$ cup Marsala wine

$\frac{1}{4}$ cup minced fresh parsley

1 cube beef bouillon

On a cutting board, with a meat mallet or the dull edge of a kitchen knife, pound each steak to about a $\frac{1}{8}$-inch thickness. Cut steak into pieces that are 2 × 4 inches. In a pie plate, beat the egg with the milk. Combine bread crumbs, Parmesan cheese, salt, and pepper on a sheet of waxed paper. Dip the meat in the egg mixture then coat with the bread crumb mixture. In a 12-inch skillet over medium high heat, melt 2 tablespoons of the butter. Cook the garlic and one third of the meat until the meat is lightly browned. Remove to a platter and keep warm. Repeat this with the remaining meat, using 6 tablespoons of butter in all. Discard the garlic. In a cup, mix the water with the flour. Melt the remaining 2 tablespoons of butter in the skillet. Add the flour mixture, Marsala wine, parsley, and bouillon cube. Cook, stirring, and as you stir, scrape up all the browned bits of the meat off the bottom, until thickened. Pour sauce over the meat before serving.

• *6 servings*

Ana's Beef Sirloin

Lomo Saltado • *Peru*

This steak may be served with French fries and white rice or you can make a sandwich out of the sirloin.   —Ana

½ pound sirloin steak, cut into
  1-inch pieces

1 garlic clove, minced

¼ teaspoon cumin

¾ cup plus 1 teaspoon olive oil

Salt and pepper

2 medium sweet onions, sliced

1 large tomato, chopped

1 red bell pepper, seeded and sliced

In a small bowl marinate the beef with garlic, cumin, 1 teaspoon oil, and salt and pepper to taste. Let set for about 1 hour. Heat the ¾ cup oil in a frying pan and cook beef until browned, stirring occasionally. When beef is cooked, add onions and cook an additional 2 minutes. Then add tomatoes and bell pepper. Cover and let sauté for 5 to 6 minutes (do not overcook; vegetables should be slightly firm).

• *2 to 4 servings*

Lilly's Meat Pie

Pastel de Carne ◆ *Argentina*

3 tablespoons olive oil

1 large onion, chopped

1 green bell pepper, seeded and
   chopped

1 jalapeño pepper, seeded and
   chopped

2 garlic cloves, minced

1 pound ground beef

¼ cup chopped black olives

2 tablespoons golden raisins

2 hard-boiled eggs, chopped

Salt and pepper

1 egg, beaten

2 tablespoons fresh grated
   Parmesan cheese

2 tablespoons Italian bread crumbs

2 pounds baking potatoes

2 to 3 tablespoons half-and-half

1 tablespoon prepared horseradish

Heat olive oil in a heavy skillet over medium heat. Add onion, both peppers, and garlic. Cook until onions are soft. Add beef and fry until brown and crumbly. Add olives, raisins, and hard-boiled eggs. Stir and season with salt and pepper to taste. Add beaten egg, Parmesan cheese, and bread crumbs. If the mixture is too thick you can add a little stock. Cook at low heat for about 20 minutes, stirring occasionally. Cook potatoes and mash

them. Add half-and-half, salt, pepper, and horseradish. Preheat oven to 350°F. Arrange meat mixture in a baking dish. Cover with the mashed potatoes and seal to the sides of the dish. Bake until done, about 45 minutes.

◆ *4 to 6 servings*

Lilly's Meat Pie

Chicken

Grilled Chicken with Mango Sauce

Pollo a la Parrilla con Salsa de Mango ◆ *Colombia*

This dish may be served with grilled vegetables and white wine.
—Nora

2 tablespoons olive oil

2 tablespoons chopped fresh
   parsley

2 garlic cloves, minced

3 tablespoons balsamic vinegar

Juice of 1 lemon

1 small jalapeño pepper, seeded
   and minced

Dried oregano

Salt and pepper

6 boneless chicken breasts

3 mangos, pitted, peeled, and
   sliced

½ cup sugar

½ cup brandy

In a bowl, combine the olive oil, parsley, garlic, and vinegar. Add lemon juice, jalapeño, and oregano to taste. Mix well and add salt and pepper to taste. Arrange the chicken in a deep bowl, cover with the marinade, and refrigerate at least 3 hours or up to 12 hours. In a bowl, combine mangos, sugar, and brandy. Mix well. Puree the mango mixture in a blender or food processor. Put the mango mixture in a saucepan and simmer at low heat until it starts to thicken. Grill the chicken breasts over medium heat or coals for 15 minutes each side until they are browned and crispy. Brush with marinade while the chicken is being cooked. Arrange the chicken on a plate or dish. Pour the mango sauce on top, making sure the chicken is covered with the sauce.

◆ *6 servings*

Chicken Cutlets in Cider-Fig Sauce

Supremas de Pollo con Salsa de Higos y Sidra ◆ *Argentina*

This dish may be served with mashed potatoes.   —Lilly

1 package (8 ounces) figs, stems removed and quartered	2 eggs
1 cup apple cider	¼ cup milk
¼ cup orange juice	½ cup flour
¼ cup sugar	1 cup Italian bread crumbs
4 boneless chicken breasts	½ cup canola oil

Place figs, cider, orange juice, and sugar in a saucepan. Simmer at low heat for about 20 minutes or until figs are tender. Preheat oven to 375°F. Flatten and tenderize each breast into a cutlet with a meat mallet. Blend the eggs into the milk. Dust each cutlet with flour, dip into the egg mixture, and dredge with bread crumbs. Heat the oil in a large skillet and fry each cutlet until golden brown on each side. Place on a baking dish. Bake for 10 minutes. Serve with the cider-fig sauce.

◆ *4 servings*

Chicken with Mushrooms

POLLO CON HONGOS ◆ *Argentina*

Serve this chicken with mashed potatoes.   —Lilly

1 roaster chicken (3 to 4 pounds), cut into 4 to 6 pieces	½ cup chopped green bell pepper
2 tablespoons olive oil	½ cup chopped roasted red bell pepper
Salt and pepper	2 cups sliced mushrooms
1 tablespoon butter	2 cups chicken gravy
½ cup chopped green onions	½ cup heavy cream

Preheat oven to 350°F. Place the chicken in a baking dish. Brush with olive oil and sprinkle with salt and pepper to taste. Bake for 30 to 40 minutes. In a saucepan, melt butter and sauté green onions and both peppers. Add mushrooms and chicken gravy. Reduce heat and simmer for 10 minutes. Lower the heat and add the cream, mixing well. Simmer for another 5 to 7 minutes. Pour sauce over the chicken pieces before serving.

◆ *4 to 6 servings*

Nora's Chicken Stew

GUISO DE POLLO ✦ *Colombia*

This Colombian stew uses local seasonings such as the herbs *guascas* or *huascas*. These can be found dried and ground in jars in Colombian markets. Included in this recipe are *papas criollas*, which are small delicious Colombian potatoes. You may be able to find both the herbs and the potatoes in Latin markets or on the Internet. You can also substitute the *papas criollas* with small, white, new potatoes.   —Nora

1 whole chicken (about 4 pounds)

4 whole green onions

4 sprigs of parsley

1 teaspoon ground *guascas*

3 cups chicken stock or water

Salt and pepper

2 pounds Idaho potatoes, peeled and cut into ¼-inch slices

2 pounds small red potatoes, peeled and sliced

1 pound *papas criollas* or small, white, new potatoes, peeled and sliced

3 hot dogs, sliced

½ cup canned peas

2 hard-boiled eggs, sliced

½ cup cream

In a large saucepan, combine chicken, green onions, parsley, *guascas*, and chicken stock or water. Add salt and pepper to taste. Bring to a boil, reduce heat, cover, and simmer gently for about 45 minutes. Let chicken cool in the broth then lift it out. Cut into 6 serving pieces and set aside. Bring the broth to a simmer over moderate heat and add all of the potatoes. Cook until they are tender. Add hot dogs, peas, and eggs. Stir mixture well. Add cream and blend well before serving.

✦ *4 to 6 servings*

Bogota Chicken Stew

POLLO BOGOTANO ◆ *Colombia*

This stew may be served with corn bread. —Nora

4 tablespoons butter

1 whole chicken (about 3 pounds),
  cut into 10 pieces

2 large onions, finely chopped

10 *papas criollas* or Idaho potatoes,
  peeled and thinly sliced

8 cups chicken stock

Salt and pepper

3 ears fresh corn, each cut
  into 3 pieces

3 tablespoons capers

2 tablespoons chopped celery

2 carrots, peeled and sliced

2 garlic cloves, minced

1 cup half-and-half

Heat butter in a flameproof casserole and sauté chicken pieces with onions until the chicken is golden on both sides. Add the potatoes and stock. Cover and cook over very low heat until the chicken is about half done and the potatoes are beginning to disintegrate, about 25 minutes. With a spoon, remove the chicken pieces to a plate and keep warm. Work the stock through a sieve; it will have been thickened by the sliced potatoes. Return the stock to the casserole and season with salt and pepper to taste. Add chicken, potatoes, corn, capers, celery, carrots, and garlic. Simmer at medium heat until all the vegetables are tender. Add the half-and-half and mix well. Cook for another 5 minutes.

◆ *4 to 6 servings*

Chicken Pie

Pastel de Pollo ◆ *Argentina*

½ cup oil

3 cups diced chicken

1 onion, chopped

1 cup chopped mushrooms

½ teaspoon tomato paste

½ cup chopped green olives

6 fresh peaches, halved

1 cup raisins

½ cup dry white wine

Pastry for 1 double-crust
   9-inch pie

3 hard-boiled eggs, halved

Sugar for dusting

Heat enough of the oil to cover the bottom of a saucepan and add the chicken pieces in batches. Fry until golden. Transfer to another dish. In the saucepan, add the rest of the oil and sauté onion and mushrooms. Cook for about 5 minutes. Add tomato paste, olives, peaches, raisins, and wine. Add the chicken and simmer for 20 minutes, stirring frequently. Preheat the oven to 350°F. Arrange one pie crust in a pie pan. Distribute the chicken mixture over it. Arrange the hard-boiled eggs over the chicken and cover with the other crust. Bake until dough is golden. Sprinkle with sugar.

◆ *4 to 6 servings*

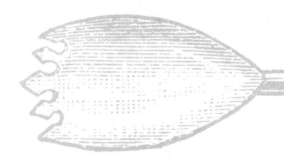

Chicken with Lentils

POLLO CON LENTEJAS ♦ *Colombia*

Lentils are the most nutritious legume in the world. Blend these little beans with chicken and you have a whole meal at little expense.   —Nora

2 cups lentils

2 garlic cloves, crushed

1 bay leaf

2 teaspoons dried oregano

Salt

¼ cup fresh lemon juice

2 pounds frying chicken, cut into bite-sized pieces and pan browned

½ cup fresh grated Parmesan cheese

1 tablespoon chopped fresh parsley

Soak lentils in 8 cups of water in a bowl for 4 to 6 hours. Place lentils, along with the water, in a pot with the garlic, bay leaf, and oregano. Add salt to taste. Simmer for about 1 hour, covered, until tender. Preheat oven to 350°F. Add the lemon juice to the lentil mixture. Place the chicken pieces in a casserole and pour the lentil mixture over them. Top with the Parmesan cheese. Bake, covered, for 1 hour. You may need to add more water during the baking. Garnish with parsley before serving.

♦ *4 to 6 servings*

Lilly's Chicken

SUPREMA DE POLLO LILLY ◆ *Argentina*

Serve this chicken on a bed of rice.   —Lilly

4 boneless chicken breasts, skinned
Salt and pepper
3 tablespoons olive oil
2 green onions, chopped
½ jalapeño pepper, seeded
    and chopped

½ cup cooked and chopped spinach
1 egg yolk
8 medium slices prosciutto
1 cup shredded mozzarella cheese
2 tablespoons melted butter

Pound the chicken breasts flat with a meat mallet. Sprinkle each breast with salt and pepper to taste. In a skillet, heat the olive oil and sauté onions, jalapeño, and spinach. Cook for 5 minutes. Add the egg yolk. Blend the ingredients and cook a few minutes longer. Preheat the oven to 350°F. Place two tablespoons of the spinach mixture on each chicken breast, spread evenly. Top with 2 slices of prosciutto. Sprinkle 2 tablespoons of mozzarella cheese on each. Roll up the chicken and secure with toothpicks. Brush with melted butter and place on a baking dish. Bake for 30 minutes.

◆ *4 servings*

Chicken with Cream

POLLO A LA CREMA ◆ *Colombia*

This dish may be served with white rice.   —Nora

3 or 4 leeks

1 tablespoon olive oil

1 garlic clove, chopped

3 to 4 cups cooked chicken, cut into
   bite-sized pieces

Salt and pepper

Pinch of nutmeg

½ cup whipping cream

1 tablespoon chopped fresh parsley

Wash the leeks thoroughly and cut into 2-inch pieces (white part only). Sauté leeks in oil along with garlic until leeks are just tender. Add chicken pieces to the pan and cook until hot. Add salt and pepper to taste, and the nutmeg. Mix well and add cream. Garnish with parsley before serving.

◆ *4 to 6 servings*

It's All in the Name

by Noemi

Despite all the years that Nohemi, Ana, Nora, and Lilly have been making Spanish dishes, swapping recipes, and learning from each other, there are still some things they cannot agree on. There are several foods in any given recipe that are referred to by different words, depending on what country you are in. Some, especially fruits and vegetables, are products of South America with its tropical weather. Even though the Spanish language was passed on to other Spanish-speaking countries from mainland Spain, the language underwent different alterations in each country. As the Spanish language encountered the language of the native peoples, new words or phrases were created and used. While cooking together in their kitchens, the four friends often debate what something is called. Here are some of the more common examples that the Latin women dispute.

- Pineapple—in Peru, Colombia, and Spain it is called *piña*, in Argentina it is called *ananá*.
- Strawberries—in Spain they are called *fresas*, in Argentina they are called *frutillas*.

- Potatoes—in Spain they are called *patatas*, in South American countries they are called *papas*.

- Corn on the cob—in Spain it is referred to as *maiz*, in South America they call it *choclo*.

- Avocado—in Peru and Argentina it is called *palta*, in Spain and Colombia it is called *aguacate*.

- Bananas—in Spain and Peru they refer to them as *plátanos*, in Argentina they call them *bananas*.

These few examples reveal how distinct each country is while still sharing a common heritage.

Lilly's Pineapple Chicken

Pollo al Ananá ◆ *Argentina*

Serve this chicken with sweet potatoes.　—Lilly

1 whole chicken (3 to 4 pounds),
　cut into 8 pieces
Salt and pepper
1 tablespoon flour
2 tablespoons butter

½ cup chopped green onions
1 fresh pineapple, peeled, cored,
　and cut into ¼-inch slices
1 cup of Marsala or port wine
1 cup pineapple juice

Preheat oven to 350°F. Season chicken with salt and pepper to taste. Dust chicken with flour. Heat the butter in a saucepan. Add onions and pineapple slices. Cook until the pineapple is golden. Add wine, pineapple juice, and the chicken, stirring frequently until the chicken is browned. Pour the mixture into a baking dish or roasting pan. Bake for 40 minutes.

◆ *6 to 8 servings*

Ana's Pineapple Chicken

POLLO EN PIÑA ◆ *Peru*

This dish may be served with rice.   —Ana

4 pounds chicken, cut into
   10 pieces
1 ripe pineapple, peeled, cored,
   and chopped
1 cup pineapple juice
2 medium onions, chopped
2 garlic cloves, peeled
1 cinnamon stick

2 bay leaves
1 green bell pepper, seeded
   and chopped
1 red bell pepper, seeded
   and chopped
½ cup Marsala wine or dry sherry
Salt and pepper

Put the pieces of chicken into a heavy casserole. Add the rest of the ingredients. Cover and simmer until the chicken is done, about 45 minutes.

◆ *4 to 6 servings*

Lime and Oregano Chicken

Pollo con Jugo de Lima y Orégano ◆ *Colombia*

Serve this chicken with boiled red potatoes.   —Nora

1 chicken (about 3 pounds), cut into 10 pieces	1 tablespoon dried oregano
2 tablespoons olive oil	3 tablespoons fresh lime juice
	Pepper

Preheat oven to 375°F. Place the chicken pieces in an oiled baking dish and mix with olive oil, oregano, lime juice, and pepper. Bake for 45 minutes or until the chicken is golden and tender.

◆ *4 to 6 servings*

Pan Chicken and Potatoes

Pollo Salteado con Papas ◆ *Argentina*

4 medium potatoes, sliced
   ¼ inch thick
3 tablespoons olive oil
1 pound boned and skinned
   chicken breast, cut into
   ½-inch strips
2 garlic cloves, minced
½ jalapeño pepper, seeded
   and chopped

1 red bell pepper, seeded
   and chopped
¼ teaspoon dried rosemary,
   crumbled
Salt and pepper
Oregano
½ cup crumbled feta cheese

Cook the potatoes in boiling water until they are tender. Add olive oil to a skillet and brown the chicken, garlic, and both peppers. Cook for 10 minutes. Add the cooked potatoes and rosemary. Sauté until potatoes are browned. Season with salt, pepper, and oregano to taste. Add the feta cheese and mix well before serving.

◆ *4 to 6 servings*

...mi's Garlic Chicken

...L Ajillo ◆ *Spain*

T his is one of my family's favorite chicken recipes. No matter how much
I make, they always want more! —Nohemi

1 chicken (about 3 pounds), cut
  into 2-inch pieces
5 garlic cloves, peeled
Salt and pepper

5 tablespoons olive oil
5 tablespoons chopped fresh
  parsley

Place chicken in a bowl. In a garlic press, smash the garlic cloves with salt
and pepper to taste. Add this to the chicken along with the oil and parsley.
Mix well and cover. Marinate in the refrigerator for at least 12 hours. Grill
the chicken over hot coals or on a gas grill, 10 minutes per side or until
done.

◆ *4 to 6 servings*

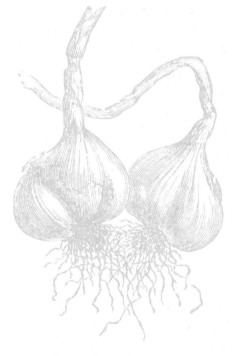

Hunter Chicken

Pollo a la Cazadora ◆ *Argentina*

Serve this chicken and vegetable dish over pasta.   —Lilly

2 tablespoons olive oil

2 pounds chicken, cut into
   10 pieces

1 cup chopped onions

1 cup seeded and sliced green
   bell pepper

1 cup chopped celery

1 can (16 ounces) chunky tomatoes

1 cup chopped mushrooms

½ cup red wine

Heat oil in a large skillet. Add chicken and cook over medium heat on both sides until lightly browned. Remove chicken from pan and put on a platter. In same skillet, add onions, bell pepper, celery, tomatoes, and mushrooms. Cook for 4 or 5 minutes or until vegetables are tender. Return the chicken to the skillet. Add red wine. Lower the heat and simmer for 45 minutes or until chicken is done, stirring the skillet occasionally.

◆ *4 to 6 servings*

Chicken in Oil and Vinegar

ESCABECHE DE POLLO ◆ *Peru*

This dish may be served hot as a main dish or cool as an appetizer.
—Ana

10 medium potatoes, peeled
    and halved
Salt and pepper
2 pounds chicken, cut into
    10 pieces
3 medium sweet onions, sliced
2 medium carrots, sliced
1 yellow bell pepper, seeded
    and sliced

¾ cup oil
½ cup white vinegar
1 head lettuce
½ cup black olives, halved
3 hard-boiled eggs, sliced
    into rings

Place potatoes in boiling water with a pinch of salt and cook until they are done. Drain potatoes and transfer to a shallow serving dish to cool. Add salt and pepper to taste to the chicken pieces. Boil chicken in a small pan with 2 cups of water until tender. Remove chicken and cool. In a large skillet, fry the chicken until browned. In a large pan, cook onions, carrots, and bell pepper in ¼ cup water for 4 to 5 minutes. Drain vegetables. Add oil, vinegar, salt and pepper to taste, and let cook at low heat until vegetables are tender. Add chicken and cook an additional 2 minutes. In a shallow serving dish, place the potatoes on a bed of cleaned and dried lettuce. Place the chicken mixture over potatoes and garnish with olives and hard-boiled eggs.

◆ *8 to 10 servings*

Napoleon Chicken

Suprema de Pollo a la Napolitana • *Argentina*

Th ese cutlets may be served with boiled or fried potatoes. —Lilly

6 boneless chicken breasts	¼ cup oil
Salt and pepper	1 cup tomato sauce
2 eggs	6 slices Virginia ham, medium-
¼ cup milk	sliced
½ cup flour	6 slices mozzarella cheese
1 cup Italian bread crumbs	Dash of oregano

Flatten the chicken breasts with a mallet and season with salt and pepper to taste. Blend the eggs with the milk. Dust each cutlet with flour. Dip into the egg mixture and dredge with bread crumbs. Heat the oil in a large skillet and fry each cutlet to golden brown on each side. Place on baking sheets. Preheat oven to 350°F. Pour the tomato sauce on top. Place one slice of ham and one slice of mozzarella cheese on each breast. Sprinkle with oregano. Bake for 8 minutes or until cheese is melted.

• *6 servings*

Pan-Fried Chicken

Pollo Salteado • *Colombia*

This chicken may be served with mashed potatoes.   —Nora

2 tablespoons olive oil

2 pounds chicken breasts, skinned, boned, and cut into ½-inch strips

2 garlic cloves, chopped

4 green onions, chopped

1 green bell pepper, seeded and chopped

½ jalapeño pepper, seeded and chopped

¼ cup Marsala wine

¼ cup fresh lemon juice

2 cups chopped mushrooms

Salt and pepper

Heat a large frying pan. Add oil, chicken, garlic, and green onions. Add both peppers. Sauté until chicken is lightly browned and tender. Remove chicken from the pan. Add Marsala wine and lemon juice. Add mushrooms and allow the liquid to reduce for a moment. Return the chicken to the hot pan and add salt and pepper to taste. Do not overcook.

◆ *4 to 6 servings*

Chicken Crepes

PANQUEQUES DE POLLO ◆ *Argentina*

Serve these crepes with a light tomato sauce.   —Lilly

Crepes

1 cup flour
¼ teaspoon salt
2 tablespoons olive oil

1 cup milk
¼ cup soda water or beer
3 eggs

Filling

4 strips smoked or Canadian bacon
1 onion, chopped
½ green bell pepper, seeded and
    chopped
1 garlic clove, chopped

1 cup chopped cooked spinach
1 cup diced cooked chicken
1 cup ricotta cheese
½ cup small curd cottage cheese
2 eggs

Assembly

2 eggs
¾ cup milk

3 cups Italian bread crumbs
Vegetable oil

To make the crepes, sift flour and salt together. In a bowl, blend oil, milk, and soda water or beer. Beat in the eggs and then blend mixture into the flour. Beat until smooth. To cook the crepes, spread 3 tablespoons of the batter in a lightly buttered skillet or crepe pan. Cook for one minute or less and turn the crepes over and cook one minute longer. The crepes should be golden and blistery.

To make the filling, heat a heavy skillet to medium heat. Add the strips of bacon and sauté until they are crispy. Remove. In the bacon drippings, sauté onion, bell pepper, and garlic. Chop the bacon into pieces and add to the mixture. Cook for 5 minutes. Add spinach, chicken, and cheeses. Add the 2 eggs. Simmer for another 7 minutes at a low temperature.

To assemble the crepes, ladle a little of the mixture into each crepe and roll. Beat the remaining 2 eggs with the milk. Dip the crepes in the egg mixture and dredge with the bread crumbs. Pour oil into a pan to a depth of 2 or 3 inches. Heat to 360°F and fry the crepes in small batches. Keep warm in heated oven until all the crepes are done.

♦ *4 to 6 servings*

Seafood

HOW THEY MET

by Noemi

Nohemi, Ana, Nora, and Lilly all ended up in eastern Ohio, an area with very little cultural diversity. One by one they met each other through various circumstances. Nora and Ana met through a mutual friend who knew both of them and introduced the two women. For several years they owned a consignment shop together which sold South American crafts and accessories. Lilly's husband's daughter came into the store and once she began speaking with the proprietors and realized that they were from Spanish-speaking countries, she brought her stepmother, Lilly, to meet them. Nohemi and Ana met because Nohemi's husband and Ana's brother-in-law worked at the same company. The men began talking and realized they both had family members that spoke Spanish. Ana had a summer picnic and she invited Lilly, Nora, Nohemi and their families. Lilly and Nohemi met at the picnic. Throughout the years the four women have had a few other members in the group. Marisa, from Argentina, spent many years in eastern Ohio before moving back to her native country with her family. The four friends still correspond with Marisa. Another friend, Eva, from Puerto Rico, was a member of the group for many years. I remember that Eva and her husband lived by a lake and had a wonderful speedboat. In the summer we would all gather there, go boating, and have wonderful picnics by the shore. Sadly, Eva was killed in a car accident several years ago. The four friends have formed a close bond for almost twenty-five years and they continue to celebrate milestones together, sharing their recipes, cultural connection, and lives.

Ana's Baked Red Snapper

Pescado al Horno ◆ *Peru*

This fish may be served with boiled potatoes or rice.   —Ana

1 whole red snapper (3 pounds),
   cleaned and boned

Salt and pepper

1 pound red onions, sliced

1 large tomato, sliced

¼ cup fresh lemon juice

½ cup fish stock or clam juice

4 tablespoons butter

½ cup cream

Preheat oven to 350°F. Rinse the fish and pat dry with paper towels. Season with salt and pepper to taste. In a buttered baking dish, lay the fish so it fits snugly in the dish. Add onions and tomato. Combine lemon juice and fish stock and pour over fish. Dot fish with butter and bake for 20 minutes. Lift the fish onto a platter. Pour cream into the dish where you cooked the fish. Blend the juices and pour over the fish.

◆ *4 to 6 servings*

Nora's Baked Red Snapper

PESCADO AL HORNO ✦ *Colombia*

Colombia has two seacoasts, one in the Pacific and the other in the Caribbean. These two coasts give the country a large choice of fish and shellfish, both of which are frequently found in the Colombian diet. This red snapper can be served with white rice.   —Nora

1 red snapper (3 to 4 pounds),
   cleaned and boned
Salt and pepper
¼ cup fresh lime juice

1 cup fish stock
4 tablespoons butter
½ cup light cream

Preheat oven to 375°F. Rinse fish and pat dry with paper towels. Season fish inside and out with salt and pepper to taste. Grease a shallow casserole with butter and arrange the fish in it. Combine lime juice and fish stock and pour over fish. Dot fish with 2 tablespoons of the butter and bake for about 30 minutes or until fish is flaky. Lift the fish onto a serving plate and keep warm. Pour the liquid from the casserole into a small saucepan. Stir in the cream and simmer at low heat. Add the remaining 2 tablespoons of the butter and blend.

✦ *4 to 6 servings*

Nora's Baked Red Snapper

Scalloped Fish

PESCADO AL GRATIN ◆ *Peru*

Peru has a rich variety of seafood that comes from the Pacific Coast thanks to El Niño, which warms the temperature of the water. Fish is greatly consumed by Peruvians and their rich recipes reflect this taste.
  —Ana

3 cups half-and-half

2 green onions, chopped

1 bay leaf

2 parsley sprigs

5 to 6 peppercorns

6 tablespoons butter

5 tablespoons flour

1 egg, beaten

Salt and pepper

1½ cups coarse cracker crumbs

1 pound white fish fillets (sole, cod, or bass), diced

1 pound sea scallops

Bring the half-and-half to a boil with the green onions, bay leaf, parsley, and peppercorns. Remove from heat and let stand 5 minutes to infuse the flavors. Melt 4 tablespoons of the butter. Stir in the flour, then stir in the half-and-half mixture. Bring to a boil, whisking constantly. Reduce heat and simmer until thickened. Remove the pan from the heat. Add the beaten egg. Mix well. Season with salt and pepper to taste. Preheat oven to 350°F. Scatter about one third of the cracker crumbs over the bottom of a buttered baking dish. Cover with a layer of the fish and the sea scallops. Spoon the sauce over the fish. Arrange the remaining two thirds of the cracker crumbs over the surface. Dot with the remaining 2 tablespoons butter. Bake until bubbling around the edges and lightly browned on top.

◆ *4 to 6 servings*

Haddock with Tomato

MERLUZA CON TOMATE ◆ *Spain*

Olive oil is a staple in Mediterranean cooking. It is even used as dressing mixed with vinegar and as a dipping sauce for bread when mixed with black pepper. Olive oil is a monosaturated fat that lowers a person's low-density lipoprotein and keeps arteries clear. The use of olive oil has been found to lower the incidence of heart disease. Twenty percent of the world's olive oil production occurs in the Andalucia region of Spain.
—Noemi

6 haddock fillets (about 2 pounds)	1 large onion, sliced
1 tablespoon olive oil	3 ripe tomatoes, thickly sliced
Salt	1 cup shredded Swiss cheese

Preheat oven to 325°F. Wash the fish fillets and pat dry with paper towels. Pour olive oil into a baking dish and arrange the fish fillets in it. Add salt to taste, and drip some oil over each fillet. Cover with onion and tomatoes. Sprinkle grated Swiss cheese on top and bake for 25 minutes or until the fish is done.

◆ *6 servings*

Haddock with Red Sauce

Pescado con Salsa Roja ◆ *Argentina*

6 medium tomatoes, peeled
and coarsely chopped

½ teaspoon dried oregano

½ teaspoon dried thyme

½ teaspoon dried basil

1 teaspoon dried chives

2 green onions, chopped

⅓ cup vermouth

6 haddock fillets (about 2 pounds)

Salt and pepper

1 teaspoon olive oil

Combine tomatoes, all herbs, onions, and vermouth in a medium saucepan. Simmer for 5 minutes. Preheat oven to 350°F. Place haddock fillets on a greased baking dish. Season with salt and pepper to taste. Arrange tomato mixture on top of fillets. Sprinkle olive oil on top. Bake for 20 minutes or until fish flakes easily.

◆ *4 to 6 servings*

◆

Lilly's Easter Dinner

MAIN

Haddock with Red Sauce 201
Pescado con Salsa Roja

SIDE

Brussels Sprouts with
Almonds 105
*Repollito de Bruselas con
Almendras*

DESSERT

Lemon Curd Pie 253
Pastel de Limón

WINE

Dry White Bordeaux

◆ ◆ ◆

Bass Marinated in Lime Juice

SEVICHE DE CORVINA ◆ *Peru*

This recipe is fish that is "cooked" in lime juice. The idea originated in the South Pacific and found its way to Latin America. In Peru it is served with sweet potatoes, corn, and lettuce.   —Ana

1 pound (about 6) fillets of striped
    bass or similar fish
Salt and pepper
1 large onion, sliced
1 jalapeño pepper, chopped
1 cup fresh lime juice

½ cup fresh lemon juice
½ pound sweet potatoes, peeled
    and sliced
1 pound white potatoes
1 tablespoon chopped fresh parsley

Put fish into a large bowl and season with salt and pepper to taste. Add onion, jalapeño, lime juice, and lemon juice. Mix, cover, and refrigerate for 3 hours or until the fish is opaque, or "cooked" by the juice. In a saucepan with water, cook sweet and regular potatoes until tender. Drain and reserve. Arrange some lettuce leaves in a nice dish. Put the fish on the platter. Lay the sweet and regular potato slices around the fish. Garnish with the parsley before serving.

◆ *4 to 6 servings*

Molinera's Sole

Lenguados Molinera ◆ *Spain*

½ cup olive oil

6 sole or flounder fillets
   (about 2 pounds)

Salt

1 cup flour

2 tablespoons chopped fresh
   parsley

¾ cup butter

Juice of 1 lemon

Lemon wedges

In a skillet over medium heat, heat oil, but not too hot. (The fish must be done inside before turning golden on the outside.) Salt fillets to taste and dredge in flour. Fry two fillets at a time until golden. Place on a serving platter and sprinkle with parsley. In a small saucepan, melt butter without boiling it. Add lemon juice and pour over fillets. Serve with lemon wedges.

◆ *6 servings*

Ana's Stuffed Sole

Lenguado Relleno ◆ *Peru*

Serve these crabmeat-stuffed fillets over rice.   —Ana

1 package (10 ounces) frozen
    spinach

2 tablespoons olive oil

1 medium onion, chopped

2 tablespoons chopped green bell
    pepper

1 garlic clove, minced

½ pound cooked crabmeat,
    fresh or canned

1 tablespoon chopped fresh parsley

1 egg, beaten

Salt and pepper

6 sole or flounder fillets (about
    2 pounds)

½ cup chicken stock

½ cup light cream

¾ cup shredded Cheddar cheese

Defrost spinach in the microwave. Drain and reserve. In a saucepan heat olive oil. Add onion, bell pepper, and garlic. Sauté for 2 minutes at low heat. If using canned crabmeat, drain. Remove cartilage. Add crabmeat and spinach. Add parsley and the beaten egg. Season with salt and pepper to taste. Preheat oven to 350°F. Sprinkle fillets with salt and pepper. Spoon crabmeat mixture on fillets. Roll up and fasten with a toothpick and place in a greased baking dish. Pour chicken stock over rolled fillets and bake for 20 minutes. Pour cream and sprinkle cheese on top of fillets and cook for another 5 minutes.

◆ *6 servings*

Peruvian Cod

PESCADO A LA PERUANA ◆ *Peru*

2 tablespoons olive oil

1 Spanish onion, chopped

1 green bell pepper, peeled, seeded, and chopped

½ jalapeño pepper, seeded and chopped

1 cup sliced mushrooms

1 garlic clove, minced

1 bay leaf

1 can (16 ounces) stewed tomatoes

Salt and pepper

Dash of oregano

4 to 6 cod fillets

Heat oil until a haze forms above the skillet. Add onion, both peppers, mushrooms, and garlic. Sauté until limp. Add bay leaf and tomatoes. Reduce heat, cover, and simmer for 30 minutes. Remove bay leaf. Season with salt and pepper to taste and the oregano. Preheat oven to 350°F. Arrange fillets in a greased baking dish. Pour sauce on top of fillets. Bake for 40 minutes or until the fish flakes easily.

◆ *4 to 6 servings*

Dry Cod in Garlic

BACALAO AL AJO ARRIERO ◆ *Spain*

2 pounds dry cod, cut into small
   pieces

5 tablespoons olive oil

1 large onion, chopped

1 cup chopped green bell pepper

6 garlic cloves, chopped

3 ripe tomatoes, peeled and
   chopped

½ cup white wine

1 cup pimientos

Place cod in a bowl and cover with cold water. Soak overnight. Wash cod in water, twice, then drain. In a skillet, heat oil. Add onion, bell pepper, and garlic. Fry on low heat, stirring, for about 10 minutes. Add the tomatoes and cod, stirring lightly. Add wine and shake the pan to mix. Cook for 10 minutes and add pimientos. Shake and simmer for 30 minutes longer or until fish is tender.

◆ *4 to 6 servings*

Fried Fish with Red Wine

Pescado en Vino Tinto ◆ *Colombia*

This dish may be served with rice.   —Nora

2 pounds fish fillet steak (such as
   snapper or bass), cut into
   4 pieces
Salt and pepper
Flour for dredging
¼ cup vegetable oil
2 medium onions, chopped

2 garlic cloves, minced
4 medium tomatoes, peeled
   and chopped
1 bay leaf
Pinch of cayenne
Pinch of ground allspice
1 cup red wine

Season fish steaks with salt and pepper to taste and coat lightly with flour, shaking to remove the excess. Heat oil in a skillet and sauté fish until it is browned on both sides. Transfer to a platter and keep warm. In oil remaining in the pan (add a little more if necessary) sauté onions and garlic until the onions are soft. Add tomatoes, bay leaf, cayenne and allspice. Add salt and pepper to taste and sauté, stirring the entire time. When the mixture is thick and well blended, stir in the wine. Bring to a simmer. Add fish and simmer for 2 to 3 minutes. Transfer fish to a plate or serving dish and pour sauce over it.

◆ *4 servings*

Baked Tuna Steak

Atún al Horno • *Peru*

4 tuna steaks (each about 8 ounces)

Salt and pepper

4 to 5 tablespoons olive oil

½ cup sliced green onions,
   including some tops

1 tablespoon chopped fresh parsley

2 tomatoes, chopped

Lime wedges

Preheat oven to 350°F. Sprinkle tuna with salt and pepper to taste. Place tuna in a single layer in a baking dish. Brush with olive oil, coating heavily. Sprinkle green onions on top. Bake, uncovered, for about 30 minutes or until the fish flakes easily. Remove to a serving dish. Sprinkle with parsley and garnish with tomatoes and lime wedges.

◆ 4 servings

Fish in Oil and Vinegar

PESCADO EN ESCABECHE ◆ *Peru*

This recipe is very popular throughout South America, although the cooking technique is different from country to country. Its origin is unknown. Some claim that it came from Portugal, others claim it came from Spain.   —Ana

3 pounds bass or red snapper, cut
   into 6 fillets
Salt
Flour for dredging
1 tablespoon butter
1 cup canola oil

3 medium onions, sliced into rings
1 or 2 green bell peppers, seeded
   and cut into strips
2 garlic cloves, chopped
¼ teaspoon dried oregano
½ cup white vinegar

Season fish with salt to taste. Dredge in flour, shaking to remove excess. Heat butter in a skillet and sauté fillets until they are browned. Transfer the cooked fish to a shallow serving dish and keep warm. Heat oil in a medium saucepan. Add onions, peppers, and garlic. Cook at low heat until vegetables are tender and browned. Stir in oregano and cook for 2 more minutes. Pour in vinegar. Stir and pour over fish just before serving.

◆ *6 servings*

Grilled Salmon with Lemon Butter

SALMON A LA PARRILLA CON MANTECA ◆ *Peru*

4 salmon steaks, each 1 inch thick

2 tablespoons melted butter

1 tablespoon fresh lemon juice

1 tablespoon chopped fresh dill

Lemon butter (recipe follows)

Combine melted butter, lemon juice, and dill. Brush salmon with the mixture. Grill salmon steaks on a charcoal barbecue grill. Grill for about 12 minutes, basting with butter mixture. When done, top each steak with a pat of lemon butter (see below).

Lemon Butter

This butter must be made 8 hours in advance of serving.   —Ana

4 tablespoons butter at room
    temperature

1 tablespoon chopped fresh parsley

2 garlic cloves, chopped

1 teaspoon chopped fresh basil

2 green onions, finely chopped

2 tablespoons fresh lemon juice

Combine all ingredients. Beat with an electric mixer until well blended. Place on a piece of plastic wrap. Form into a 3 × 3-inch square, using a spatula. Wrap with plastic and refrigerate for 8 hours.

◆ *4 servings*

Fish Stew

GUISO DE PESCADO ◆ *Colombia*

This stew may be served with boiled potatoes.   —Nora

3 pounds sole fillets or any
   white fish
4 tablespoons olive oil
2 medium onions, chopped
1 or 2 jalapeño peppers, seeded
   and chopped

3 medium tomatoes, peeled
   and chopped
¼ cup fresh lemon juice

Cut fish into 2-inch pieces and place in large bowl. Heat 2 tablespoons of the oil in a skillet and add the onions, peppers, and tomatoes. Cook until onions are soft. Add lemon juice. Remove from heat and set aside. In another skillet, add the remaining 2 tablespoons of oil and fry fish until lightly browned. Remove to a platter. Return skillet with onion, pepper, and tomato mixture to the stove at low heat. Add pieces of fish and simmer for 20 minutes.

◆ *4 to 6 servings*

Ana's Fisherman Stew

GUISO DE PESCADOR ◆ *Peru*

6 slices Canadian bacon, cut into
  strips
1 tablespoon olive oil
1 large onion, chopped
1 green bell pepper, seeded and
  chopped
½ jalapeño pepper, seeded and
  chopped
½ cup chopped celery
1 garlic clove, chopped
2 cups tomatoes, peeled, seeded,
  and crushed

2 cups fish or chicken stock
½ cup dry white wine
2 cups peeled and diced potatoes
2 carrots, diced
1 pound white fish (cod or
  flounder), skinned and cut
  into chunks
10 medium sea scallops
1 pound large or jumbo shrimp,
  peeled and deveined
Salt and pepper

Fry the Canadian bacon in a large pan over medium heat until browned, but
crisp. Remove and drain on paper towels. Pour off all but 1 tablespoon of fat.
Add olive oil to the pan and cook the onion, both peppers, and celery, stirring occasionally until all the vegetables are soft. Add garlic, tomatoes,
stock, and wine. Bring to a boil. Reduce heat. Cover and simmer for 15 minutes. Add potatoes and carrots. Cover and simmer for 10 minutes or until
the potatoes are tender. Add chunks of fish, bacon, sea scallops, and shrimp.
Simmer gently, uncovered, until fish, scallops, and shrimp are cooked, about
15 minutes. Salt and pepper to taste before serving.

◆ *6 to 8 servings*

Marinated Shrimp

CAMARONES MARINADOS ◆ *Peru*

2 pounds medium shrimp, peeled and deveined	1 green bell pepper, seeded and chopped
2 cups bitter orange juice	1 tablespoon chopped fresh parsley
1 medium onion, chopped	1 teaspoon dried basil
1 jalapeño pepper, seeded and minced	1 large tomato, chopped
	Salt and pepper

Drop shrimp into a large saucepan of boiling water and boil for 2 minutes. Drain and mix with orange juice, onion, and both peppers. Add parsley, basil, and tomato. Season with salt and pepper to taste. Let stand 1 hour before serving.

◆ *4 to 6 servings*

Colombian Shrimp

CAMARONES LATINOS ◆ *Colombia*

These easy-to-prepare shrimp may be served with pasta or rice.
    —Nora

4 tablespoons butter

1 pound medium shrimp, peeled
    and deveined

2 garlic cloves, minced

¼ cup chopped fresh parsley

1 tablespoon fresh lemon juice

Salt and pepper

Heat butter in a pan. Add shrimp, garlic, parsley, and lemon juice. Cook
until shrimp are tender, about 15 minutes. Add salt and pepper to taste.

◆ *4 to 6 servings*

Tasty shrimp on a plate

Shrimp with Garlic and Lemon

Camarón a la Brocheta con Salsa de Limón ◆ *Peru*

Serve these broiled shrimp with a green salad.   —Ana

½ cup butter

½ cup olive oil

3 garlic cloves, minced

3 tablespoons chopped fresh
  parsley

2 tablespoons fresh lemon juice

2 pounds medium shrimp, peeled,
  deveined, and skewered

Lemon wedges

Melt butter in a skillet. Add oil, garlic, parsley, and lemon juice. Heat just until bubbling, then remove the sauce from the heat. Place the skewered shrimp on a rack in a pan. Brush generously with garlic sauce. Broil the shrimp 4 inches from the heat until they turn bright pink. Baste at least once with the garlic sauce. Turn and broil the other side for about 3 minutes. Garnish with lemon wedges.

◆ *4 to 6 servings*

Shrimp in Coconut Sauce

LANGOSTINOS CON CREMA DE COCO ◆ *Colombia*

This shrimp and fish dish may be served with rice.   —Nora

1 cup dried shrimp

¼ cup plus 2 tablespoons olive oil

2 medium onions, grated

2 garlic cloves, crushed

1 cup cashew nuts or almonds, ground

1 cup fresh bread crumbs

4 cups coconut milk

1 bass fillet or any white fish (3 or 4 pounds)

1 pound small shrimp, peeled and deveined

Soak dried shrimp in warm water for 10 minutes. Drain shrimp, then puree in blender or food processor. Set aside. Heat the ¼ cup olive oil in a heavy skillet and sauté onions, garlic, nuts, and the shrimp puree for 5 minutes. Stir in bread crumbs and coconut milk and simmer, stirring occasionally until the mixture is thick. In another skillet, heat the 2 tablespoons of olive oil. Sauté fillet lightly. Add fresh shrimp and sauté for 2 to 4 minutes or until shrimp turns pink. Fold the shrimp and fish mixture into coconut milk sauce.

◆ *4 to 6 servings*

Rice Shrimp Sauté

Arroz Salteado con Langostinos ♦ *Peru*

4 tablespoons butter
½ onion, chopped
½ green bell pepper, seeded and
  chopped
1 teaspoon chopped jalapeño
  pepper

1 pound large shrimp, peeled and
  deveined
2 cups cooked long-grain rice
Salt and pepper

In a heavy skillet over medium heat, melt 2 tablespoons of the butter. Add onion and both peppers. Cook for 5 minutes. Add shrimp. Cook 2 to 4 minutes, until shrimp turn pink and are cooked through. Add cooked rice and the remaining 2 tablespoons of butter. Mix well and heat through. Add salt and pepper to taste before serving.

♦ *4 to 6 servings*

Rice with Shellfish

ARROZ CON MARISCOS ◆ *Peru*

This is a popular dish in Peru, flavorful when blended with rice and a rich mixture of shellfish.   —Ana

4 tablespoons olive oil

1 large onion, finely chopped

2 green bell peppers, seeded and
   cut into strips

1 jalapeño pepper, seeded and cut
   into strips

2 garlic cloves, minced

2 cups long-grain rice

4 cups shrimp stock

2 tablespoons chopped fresh
   parsley

½ pound medium shrimp

½ pound whole scallops

12 clams

12 oysters

Heat 2 tablespoons of oil in a heavy skillet. Sauté onion, both peppers, and garlic. Cook until tender. Remove and transfer to a flameproof casserole. Add the remaining 2 tablespoons of oil to the skillet. Add rice and sauté until rice has absorbed the oil, taking care not to let it brown. Transfer rice to the casserole. Add shrimp stock to the rice. Bring to a boil over high heat. Reduce the heat to low and cook, uncovered, until the rice is tender and all the liquid is absorbed, about 20 minutes. Add parsley, shrimp, scallops, clams, and oysters. Blend everything together. Cook covered for about 3 minutes. Stir, making sure that the mixture is well blended. Serve immediately.

◆ *4 to 6 servings*

Marinated Mussels

MEJILLONES CON SALSA ◆ *Spain*

When I was a young woman, there was a bar in León where, apart from drinks, the only food offered as *tapas* was mussels. The mussels were made with all kinds of sauces, from mayonaise, to tomato, to herb sauces. Even just steamed with lemon juice on top. It was one of my favorite places to stop by when my friends and I were hopping bars. —Nohemi

½ cup white wine

¼ cup chopped onion

1½ pounds mussels, scrubbed
    and debearded

2 tablespoons olive oil

3 garlic cloves, minced

1 tablespoon minced fresh thyme

1 tablespoon minced fresh parsley

2 bay leaves

3 tablespoons red wine vinegar

1 teaspoon paprika

Pinch of cayenne

In a large saucepan, bring wine and onion to a boil. Add mussels. Cover and steam for about 5 minutes or until mussels open. Transfer mussels to a plate. Save the cooking liquid. Heat olive oil in a skillet over medium heat. Add garlic and sauté for 2 minutes. Add thyme, parsley, and bay leaves and sauté for 1 minute. Add the cooking liquid from the mussels, then the vinegar, paprika, and cayenne. Remove mussels from the shell, reserving one half of each shell. Place mussels in a large bowl and pour marinade over them. Cover and refrigerate for 2 hours. Place reserved mussel half shells on a serving plate. Scoop a mussel into each shell. Pour marinade over the mussels before serving.

◆ *4 to 6 servings*

Oysters in Lime Juice

Ostras en Jugo de Lima ◆ *Peru*

4 dozen oysters, shucked

1 cup fresh lime juice

3 large tomatoes, peeled
and chopped

1 large onion, chopped

1 jalapeño pepper, seeded
and chopped

2 tablespoons chopped fresh
parsley

Salt and pepper

Lettuce

Put oysters into a large bowl with lime juice. Cover and refrigerate 8 to 12 hours. Strain oysters, reserving juice. In a bowl, combine oysters with tomatoes, onion, jalapeño, and parsley. Add the reserved juice. Season with salt and pepper to taste. Line a serving dish with lettuce and pour the oyster mixture on it.

◆ *4 to 6 servings*

Clams in Marinara Sauce

ALMEJAS A LA MARINERA ◆ *Spain*

1 onion, chopped
¼ cup olive oil
1 teaspoon paprika
4 tomatoes, chopped
2 pounds clams

¼ cup white wine
Salt and pepper
1 tablespoon chopped fresh parsley
Lemon wedges

In a skillet, sauté onion in hot oil for 10 minutes and add paprika and tomatoes. Reduce heat. Stir in clams, wine, and salt and pepper to taste. Cook until clams open. Sprinkle with parsley and serve with lemon wedges.

◆ *4 to 6 servings*

Fried Squid

CALAMARES FRITOS A LA ROMANA ◆ *Spain*

Even now when I visit Spain I try to buy a *bocadillo de calamares,* a fried squid sandwich. It brings back memories of shared midafternoon snacks with friends. The batter for these fried squid must be prepared 30 minutes before you need it.   —Nohemi

2 tablespoons flour

2 tablespoons milk

1 egg, separated

2 tablespoons olive oil

1 pound squid, cut into ½-inch rings

Vegetable oil

Mix a batter from the flour, milk, egg yolk, and oil until creamy and let rest for 30 minutes. Just before using the batter, beat the egg white until stiff and fold in. Dip the squid rings in the batter, covering both sides. In a pan or deep fryer, heat about 2 inches of oil to 350°F and fry a few rings at a time. Drain on paper towels if needed.

◆ *4 to 6 servings*

Desserts

A holiday feast

A Christmas Surprise

by Noemi

When I was a child, my family always celebrated two Christmases. The first one took place on December 25th, the traditional day to celebrate in America. The second one was on January 6th, the day of the three wisemen, which is celebrated in Spain. For the Spanish celebration Mamá always made a cake and in the cake she inserted tiny pieces of foiled paper that contained numbers. Each number corresponded to a prize that was wrapped and waiting in a basket nearby. As we greedily consumed the pieces of delicious cake, we hoped that our slice contained one of the coveted foils. In Spain, instead of inserting numbered pieces of foil, traditionally a small glass figurine was hidden in the cake. Being the recipient of the slice with the hidden prize assured luck for the rest of the year. Many years I drew a foil and received a prize. Secretly, I think Mamá tried to make sure almost all the slices contained numbered pieces of foil so that no one would feel left out. My American friends loved coming over for the celebration and I always felt so lucky to celebrate Christmas and open gifts not just on one day but two!

Christmas Cake

Roscón de Reyes   •   *Spain*

2 packages dry yeast	3 eggs
¼ cup lukewarm water	1 teaspoon salt
1 cup milk	Crisco
6½ cups flour, sifted	1 tablespoon orange zest
½ pound (2 sticks) butter	1 tablespoon lemon zest
2 teaspoons cinnamon	Glazed red cherries
½ cup sugar	Confectioners' frosting

Dissolve yeast in lukewarm water and let stand 5 minutes. Scald milk. Cook to lukewarm. Add milk to yeast, along with 1 cup of the flour, and beat well. Cover and let stand 30 minutes. In a large bowl, cream butter until soft and fluffy. Gradually add cinnamon and sugar. Beat in eggs, one at a time. Add yeast mixture and beat again. Stir in salt and remaining flour to make a soft, easily handled dough. Knead dough on a lightly floured surface until smooth and elastic, about 8 minutes. Place dough in a bowl greased with Crisco. Turn once to coat with grease. Cover and let rise 1 hour or until doubled in size. On a lightly floured board, knead in orange and lemon zests. Divide dough in half and form each half into a long, narrow roll about 2 inches thick. If you choose to follow the Spanish tradition, now is the time to insert the numbered pieces of foil that correspond to gifts. Smooth out the dough where the foil is inserted. Form a circle with each, joining both ends, and place circles on a greased baking sheet. Cover and let rise until circles double in size, about 30 minutes. Meanwhile, preheat oven to 400°F. With a very sharp knife, make tiny slashes on top of the crown, about 2 inches apart. Bake for 20 minutes. Frost with confectioners' frosting and decorate with glazed cherries.

• 6 to 8 servings

Coconut Custard

Peru has three distinct climatic regions, one of which is in the Selva or Amazonian jungle basin between Peru and Brazil. There Peruvians grow many tropical fruits including the coconut, or *coco*.   —Ana

1 can (14 ounces) condensed milk

1 can (12 ounces) evaporated milk

½ cup sugar

½ cup milk

½ cup shredded fresh coconut
   (see page 30)

6 eggs

Whipped cream

Preheat oven to 350°F. Combine all ingredients, except ¼ cup of the sugar and the whipped cream, in a blender for 3 minutes. Pour mixture into a caramelized baking dish (cook the remaining ¼ cup sugar over low heat until it melts and turns golden brown). Place into a roasting pan and add enough hot water to reach halfway up the sides of the dish. Bake for 45 minutes or until a knife comes out clean. Let cool. Run the knife around the edge of the dish to separate it from the sides. Refrigerate 8 to 12 hours. Serve with whipped cream.

◆ *4 to 6 servings*

Coconut Cream

CREMA DE COCO ◆ *Peru*

For directions on handling fresh coconuts, see Cream of Coconut Soup, page 30.   —Noemi

1 medium coconut, hulled, milked, and shredded	½ cinnamon stick
1½ cups sugar	3 cups regular milk
	4 eggs, beaten

In a saucepan, combine sugar, cinnamon stick, and ½ cup of the coconut milk. Stir the mixture over low heat until the sugar is dissolved. Add 2 cups of the shredded coconut and continue to cook the mixture, stirring, until the coconut is transparent. Remove and discard the cinnamon stick. Stir in the milk, mixing thoroughly. Simmer, stirring from time to time, until the mixture is thickened. Pour ½ cup of the mixture into the eggs, beating with a whisk. Pour the egg mixture into the saucepan and cook, stirring over low heat. Do not let boil. When it is thick, remove from heat and pour into a bowl or serving dish. Refrigerate for several hours before serving.

◆ *4 to 6 servings*

Coconut Sweet

MIEL DE COCO ◆ *Peru*

For directions on handling fresh coconuts, see Cream of Coconut Soup, page 30. —Noemi

1 medium coconut, hulled, milked, and shredded

1 cup sugar

1 cup milk

1 tablespoon butter

½ teaspoon vanilla extract

Combine 1 cup of the coconut milk and the shredded coconut with the remaining ingredients and cook over medium heat, stirring constantly until the bottom of the pan shows when stirred. Serve in bowls.

◆ *4 to 6 servings*

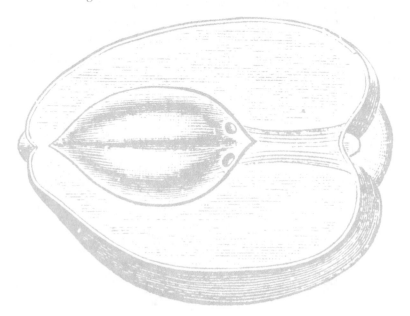

Fried Dough

BUÑUELOS ◆ *Colombia*

It was traditional at Mamá's house to have this dessert on Easter day. I can remember her making it and I know how much time it took to prepare. *Semana Santa* (Easter week) was full of prayer and food. Make the syrup first and keep it warm while you prepare the dough.   —Nora

Syrup

1½ cups brown sugar

3 cups water

1 cinnamon stick

1 clove

Dough

2 cups flour

1 tablespoon baking powder

1½ teaspoons salt

1 tablespoon sugar

1 egg, beaten

½ cup milk

2 tablespoons melted butter

Vegetable oil for frying

To make the syrup, combine all the ingredients in a pan and heat, stirring until the sugar has dissolved. Leave to simmer until the mixture has reduced to a light syrup. Remove the cinnamon stick and clove.

To make the dough, put flour, baking powder, and salt in a bowl. Stir in sugar. In a mixing bowl whisk egg and milk together. Gradually stir into the dry mixture, then beat in the melted butter to make a soft dough. Turn the dough onto a floured board and knead until it is smooth and elastic. Divide the dough into 18 pieces. Shape into 18 balls. With your hands, flatten the balls to shape ½-inch-thick disks. Use the floured handle of a wooden spoon to poke a hole through the center of each *bueñuelo*. Pour oil into a deep frying pan to a depth of 2 to 3 inches. Heat it to 375°F for 30 to 40 seconds. Fry each *buñuelo* until it is puffy and golden on both sides. Drain the *buñuelos* on a paper towel and dust them with sugar. Serve with the warm syrup.

◆ *4 to 6 servings*

Lilly's Cheesecake

Torta de Queso ◆ *Argentina*

Pastry

1 ½ cups flour

1 ¼ teaspoons baking powder

½ teaspoon salt

4 tablespoons butter, softened

¼ cup sugar

1 egg

½ teaspoon vanilla extract

½ teaspoon grated orange zest

1 tablespoon milk

1 tablespoon water

Filling

1 container (15 ounces) ricotta
   cheese

½ cup small curd cottage cheese

¼ cup sugar

3 eggs

1 ½ teaspoons flour

1 teaspoon vanilla extract

¼ cup raisins

2 tablespoons finely chopped
   citron

Assembly

1 egg yolk

To make the pastry, sift flour with baking powder and salt. In a medium bowl, with a mixer, beat butter with sugar and egg until light and creamy. Beat in vanilla, orange zest, milk, and water. Add half the flour mixture and with a wooden spoon beat until well blended. Add remaining flour mixture, mixing with your hands until the pastry leaves the side of the bowl and holds together. Turn pastry out onto a board and knead several times to blend. Cover and set aside while you make the filling.

To make the filling, in a medium bowl, beat ricotta and cottage cheeses until creamy. Add sugar, eggs, flour, vanilla, raisins, and citron. Beat until combined.

To assemble the cheesecake, preheat the oven to 350°F. Divide the pastry in half. On a clean surface, roll one half into an 11-inch circle. Fit the pastry into a pie plate. Trim to the edge of the plate. Brush bottom with egg white. Roll remaining pastry to a $\frac{1}{8}$-inch thickness. With pastry cutter, cut the pastry into 10 strips, $\frac{1}{2}$ inch wide. Pour the filling into the pie plate. Place 5 strips across the filling, pressing firmly to the edge of a pie plate. Place remaining strips across the first ones, to make the lattice. Reroll trimming and cut into $\frac{1}{2}$-inch strips. Place around the edge of the pie. Press edges with a fork. Beat egg yolk with 1 teaspoon water. Brush over crust. Place a strip of foil, about 2 inches wide, around the edge of the crust to prevent overbrowning. Bake for 50 minutes or until top is golden brown and filling is set. Cool on a rack and serve cold.

◆ *4 to 6 servings*

Sweet Potato Cheesecake

TORTA DE QUESO Y PATATA ◆ *Argentina*

2 packages (16 ounces) light cream
   cheese

1 cup sour cream

1 cup mashed, cooked sweet
   potatoes

1 cup dark brown sugar

1 large egg

2 large egg whites

2 tablespoons Grand Marnier

2 teaspoons vanilla extract

1 (9 inch) prepared graham
   cracker crust

Preheat oven to 350°F. In a large bowl, beat cream cheese and sour cream.
Add sweet potatoes and brown sugar. Add egg and egg whites one at a
time, beating after each addition. Add Grand Marnier and vanilla. Spoon
the mixture into the crust. Bake for 40 to 50 minutes or until set. Remove
from oven to cool. Refrigerate for 2 hours before serving.

◆ *4 to 6 servings*

Spanish Rice Pudding

Arroz con Leche ◆ *Spain*

This pudding may be served at room temperature, or cold during the summer.   —Nohemi

4 cups milk

Peel of ½ lemon

½ cup rice

1 cinnamon stick

½ cup sugar

1 tablespoon butter

Dash of salt

Cinnamon

In a saucepan over medium heat, bring milk and lemon peel to a boil. Add rice and cinnamon stick. Stir and cook over very low heat for about 45 minutes. Stir from time to time. Remove lemon peel and cinnamon sick. Add sugar, butter, and salt. Cook 5 minutes longer, stirring constantly. Pour into a shallow serving dish. Sprinkle with cinnamon.

◆ *4 to 6 servings*

Argentinean Rice Pudding

Arroz con Leche ◆ *Argentina*

Serve this pudding hot or cold.   —Lilly

¼ pound (1 stick) butter

4 tart apples, peeled, cored, and
  sliced

5 cups milk

1 cup long- or medium-grain
  white rice

½ cup sugar

2 cinnamon sticks

1 vanilla bean, split lengthwise

¼ teaspoon salt

½ cup Marsala or port wine

½ cup brown sugar

Pinch of cinnamon

In a heavy skillet, melt butter. Add apples and sauté until they are tender. Add a little sugar and reserve. Combine the milk, rice, sugar, cinnamon sticks, vanilla bean, and salt in a heavy medium saucepan. Bring to a boil. Reduce heat to low and cook until rice is tender and mixture is thick, stirring constantly, about 50 minutes. Mix in Marsala or port wine and brown sugar. Spoon into bowls and top with sautéed apples and cinnamon.

◆ *4 to 6 servings*

Rice Pudding with Raisins

Arroz con Leche y Pasas ◆ *Argentina*

This pudding may be served hot or cold.   —Lilly

½ cup golden raisins

¼ cup Marsala or port wine

1 cup half-and-half

1 cup water

½ cup white long-grain rice

¼ cup sugar

Dash of nutmeg

¼ teaspoon cinnamon

In a small pan, warm raisins with Marsala or port wine. Meanwhile, in a pan, blend half-and-half with water. Add rice, cover the pan, and bring to a boil, and stir. Reduce heat to low, cover, and cook for 20 minutes or until the rice is tender and creamy. Add raisin mixture and sugar. Add a dash of nutmeg and the cinnamon.

◆ *4 to 6 servings*

Spanish French Toast

Torrijas • *Spain*

*T*orrijas are traditionally served during Easter all over Spain, but especially in the region of Andalucia. Spanish bakeries display them in their windows to entice customers inside. In 2000, after being in America for twenty-five years during Easter, I was able to spend the holiday in León. My sister Maria (the great cook) was going to make *torrijas* for me, but we were so busy shopping and visiting with family and friends that we never got around to it. She still owes me some *torrijas!*   —Nohemi

Syrup

2 cups water
½ cup sugar
1 cup white wine

Toast

1 cup milk
2 large eggs, beaten
2 tablespoons sugar
Pinch of cinnamon

4 slices dried French bread, 1 inch
  thick
4 tablespoons butter
Confectioners' sugar

To make the syrup, in a heavy saucepan, boil water and sugar for 8 minutes. Add wine and boil for about 5 minutes or until it thickens. Keep warm.

To make the toast, mix the first 4 ingredients in a medium saucepan. Cook over medium heat until slightly thickened, stirring constantly, for about 2 minutes. Do not boil. Arrange bread slices in a baking dish. Pour the mixture over the bread. Let soak for 30 minutes. Melt 2 tablespoons of the butter in a skillet over medium heat. Add bread slices and cook until golden brown, 3 minutes per side. Sprinkle with confectioners' sugar, adding more of the remaining 2 tablespoons of butter if needed. Pour syrup over each toast before serving.

◆ *4 servings*

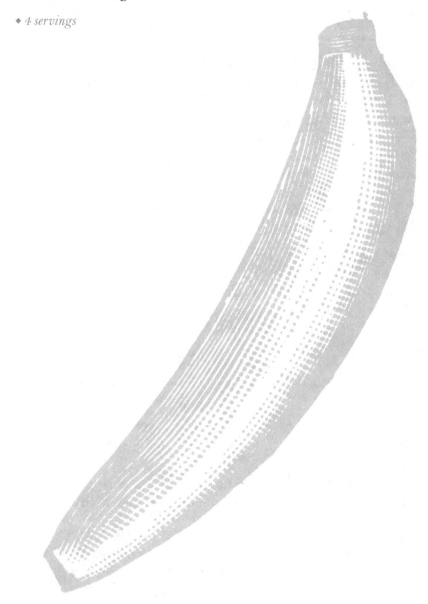

Banana and Pineapple Cake

Torta de Banana y Ananá • *Argentina*

3 cups flour

2 cups sugar

1 teaspoon salt

1 teaspoon baking soda

3 eggs, slightly beaten

2 cups mashed bananas

1 cup cooking oil

1 can crushed pineapple,
   undrained

1½ teaspoons vanilla extract

Confectioners' sugar

Preheat oven to 350°F. In a large bowl, stir flour, sugar, salt, and baking soda. Make a well in the center of the dry ingredients. Combine eggs, bananas, oil, pineapple, and vanilla. Add all wet ingredients to the center of the dry ingredients, stirring well until moistened. Pour batter into a greased and floured 10-inch fluted pan and bake for 60 minutes. Remove and cool on wire rack. Sprinkle with confectioners' sugar before serving.

• 4 to 6 servings

Bananas Baked in Rum

BANANAS AL RHUM • *Argentina*

These bananas should be served hot, with ice cream.   —Lilly

4 bananas, quartered

4 tablespoons (½ stick) butter, melted

3 tablespoons brown sugar

2 tablespoons fresh lemon juice

6 tablespoons rum

Put bananas in a small baking dish. In a small bowl, mix butter, brown sugar, lemon juice, and rum. Sprinkle over bananas, turning to coat the pieces. Bake at 400°F for 20 minutes, basting occasionally.

• *2 to 4 servings*

Almond and Chocolate Cake

Torta de Almendras y Chocolate ◆ *Peru*

Cake

4 eggs, separated

¾ cup sugar

½ teaspoon vanilla extract

2 tablespoons Cognac

6 tablespoons butter, melted and
    cooled

1 cup finely ground almonds

3 ounces semisweet chocolate,
    chopped

⅔ cup sifted flour

¼ teaspoon cinnamon

¼ teaspoon nutmeg

¼ teaspoon salt

Chocolate Glaze

10 ounces semisweet chocolate

2 tablespoons butter

To make the cake, preheat oven to 350°F. Beat egg yolks, sugar, vanilla, and Cognac in a medium bowl until slightly thickened and paler yellow. Beat egg whites in a separate bowl until stiff. Beat half the beaten egg whites into the mixture until blended. Gradually fold in the butter. Combine almonds, chocolate, flour, cinnamon, nutmeg, and salt and fold into the egg mixture alternating with the remaining beaten egg whites. Pour into a buttered 8 × 8 pan and smooth the top. Bake for 50 to 60 minutes.

To make the chocolate glaze, place chocolate and butter in a double boiler over low heat. Mix well. Once the mixture is melted, remove from heat. When the cake is cool, brush with the chocolate glaze.

◆ *4 to 6 servings*

Apples in Pastry

Manzanas de Paseo • *Argentina*

Serve this dessert warm with ice cream.   —Lilly

Pastry

3 cups flour

1 teaspoon salt

½ pound plus 2 tablespoons (2¼ sticks) butter, cold and cut into cubes

6 tablespoons lard, cold and cut into cubes

10 tablespoons ice water

Apples

¼ cup orange marmalade or raspberry preserves

2 tablespoons finely chopped almonds

2 tablespoons golden raisins

6 medium Granny Smith or Rome apples

1 lemon, halved

Assembly

2 tablespoons sugar

½ teaspoon cinnamon

1 teaspoon grated lemon zest

1 egg

To make the pastry, combine flour and salt in a large bowl. Cut in butter and lard until mixture resembles coarse meal. Gradually add water, 1 or 2 tablespoons at a time, stirring lightly with a fork between additions, until the mixture cleans the sides of the bowl. Gather the pastry into a ball, wrap in plastic wrap, and refrigerate at least for 30 minutes. Roll out pastry on a surface into a rectangle about ½ inch thick. The short side should be facing you. Fold top third of pastry over center third. Fold bottom third over top third. Turn pastry one quarter turn. Roll out again into a 12 × 7-inch rectangle, about ½ inch thick. Fold again into thirds. Refrigerate, wrapped in plastic, at least 30 minutes. Repeat the process of rolling out the pastry, folding it over, turning and rolling out again. Fold as before, wrap in plastic, and refrigerate for 30 minutes.

To make the apples, heat marmalade or preserves in a small pan over low heat, stirring, until melted. Stir in almonds and raisins. Remove from heat. Peel and core the apples. Rub apples with cut surface of lemon to prevent discoloration.

To assemble, roll out pastry on lightly floured surface into 6 squares, each about 10 × 10 inches. Place an apple in the center of each square of pastry. In a small bowl, mix the sugar and cinnamon. Sprinkle ¼ teaspoon of cinnamon sugar and lemon zest on top of each apple. Spoon rounded teaspoon of preserves and raisin mixture into each apple core. Sprinkle tops of apples with remaining cinnamon sugar mixture. Heat oven to 400°F. Beat egg with 2 tablespoons water. Brush edges of pastry with egg mixture. Fold corners of pastry up to enclose the apple, pinch corners firmly together and seal. Transfer to baking sheet. Brush lightly with egg mixture. Bake apples for 15 minutes. Reduce oven to 350°F. Bake for another 20 minutes or until pastry is golden brown.

◆ *6 servings*

Apple Fritters

Buñuelos de Manzana ◆ *Argentina*

Vegetable oil

2 eggs

1 tablespoon sugar

3 tablespoons flour

⅛ teaspoon salt

4 apples, peeled, cored, and sliced
  into ½-inch rings

Confectioners' sugar

Cinnamon

In a pan or deep fryer, heat 2 to 3 inches of oil to 350°F. Mix together eggs, sugar, flour, and salt in a bowl. Dip a few apple rings at a time into the batter and fry them in oil until they are golden brown. Place on paper towels to drain. Dust with confectioners' sugar and cinnamon before serving.

◆ *4 to 6 servings*

Cheese and Raisin Tart

Pastel de Queso y Pasas de Uvas ◆ *Peru*

Pastry

1 ½ cups flour

3 tablespoons sugar

1 teaspoon salt

¼ pound (1 stick) butter, cold
    and diced

1 egg yolk

¼ cup ice water

Filling

1 cup ricotta cheese

1 cup of farmer cheese or similar
    style cheese

3 eggs, separated

⅔ cup granulated sugar

1 tablespoon grated orange zest

3 tablespoons orange juice

4 tablespoons melted butter

¼ cup flour

⅓ cup golden raisins

2 tablespoons Cognac

To make the pastry, stir flour, sugar, and salt together. Cut in butter with 2 knives or pastry blender. Add egg yolk and ice water. Toss mixture with fork until dough begins to bind together. Wrap in plastic and refrigerate for 2 hours while preparing the filling.

To make the filling, press both cheeses in colander and drain all liquid. Place drained cheese in a bowl. Add egg yolks and ⅓ cup of the sugar. Beat with an electric mixer until light and fluffy. Add grated orange zest and orange juice and slowly add melted butter in a steady stream until well blended. Sift flour over mixture. Add raisins and Cognac. Beat egg whites with remaining ⅛ cup of sugar and fold in.

To assemble the tart, preheat oven to 350°F. Roll chilled pastry into an 11-inch circle and place into pie plate. Fold and roll the edges even with plate. Pour mixture into shell. Bake for 60 minutes or until golden. Refrigerate for 3 hours before serving.

◆ *4 to 6 servings*

Mango Cream

CREMA DE MANGO ◆ *Peru*

5 large mangos, pitted and peeled

3 tablespoons sugar

2 oranges, peeled, seeded, and cut
into small pieces

1 tablespoon fresh lemon juice

2 cups whipping cream

1 cup pecan pieces

12 red maraschino cherries

Blend mangos in a blender until smooth. Add sugar. Blend again and transfer to a bowl. Stir in oranges and lemon juice. Whip cream and fold into mango mixture. Add pecans. Serve in tall glasses. Top with maraschino cherries.

◆ 4 to 6 servings

Spanish Dough Sticks

CHURROS ♦ *Spain*

When we were children, my younger brother, Javier, and I spent two or three weeks visiting a town where Papá had some cousins. On Sundays after church, on our way back home, our cousin Petri stopped at a *churros* cart on the street and bought some *churros* to take home for breakfast. The *churros* were fried there on the street in plain sight for everyone to watch. The dough came from a machine above the frying pan in a thick string. The *"churrero"* man had a lot of dexterity and using a couple of long thick bars of metal he coiled the dough in the hot oil to accommodate as much dough as possible. Once the dough was fried, while the coil was draining, he cut it into 6-inch pieces and sprinkled them with sugar. What a treat for the eyes and the tummy!   —Nohemi

2½ cups slightly salted water or
   1¼ cups water and 1¼ cups
   milk

¾ cup sifted flour

2 eggs

Vegetable oil

Confectioners' sugar

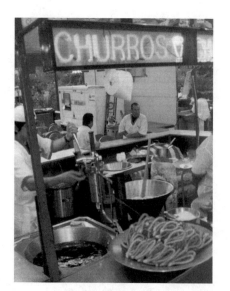

Bring water to a boil over high heat. Add flour and beat vigorously with a wooden spoon, until it no longer sticks to the pan. Remove from heat and add eggs, stirring, until the dough is smooth. Put the dough in a pastry bag with a wide fluted nozzle. In a pan or deep fryer, heat 2 to 3 inches of oil to 350°F. Squirt dough in strips of about 5 inches into the oil and deep-fry it until it is golden. Drain on paper towels and sprinkle confectioners' sugar on top before serving.

♦ *4 to 6 servings*

A typical churros *cart in Spain*

Puff Shells with Custard Sauce and Raspberry Cream

Bombas de Crema con Salsa de Fresas • *Argentina*

Puff Shells

1 cup water
¼ pound (1 stick) butter

1 cup flour
4 eggs

Custard Sauce

2 cups milk
4 egg yolks
½ cup sugar
3 tablespoons cornstarch

¼ teaspoon salt
1 teaspoon vanilla extract
2 tablespoons butter

Raspberry Sauce

2 cups fresh or frozen berries (add
　　enough water to berries to fill
　　both cups)

1 cup sugar
2 tablespoons cornstarch

To make the puff shells, preheat the oven to 400°F. Place 1 cup of water in a pan and bring it to a boil. Add butter. When butter is melted and boiling, add flour. Reduce heat and stir until it forms a ball and comes away from the sides of the pan. Remove from heat. Add eggs, one at a time, beating well after each one. Drop walnut-size rounds on a buttered cookie sheet. Bake for 40 to 45 minutes or until they are golden and dry.

To make the custard sauce, place milk in a pan and heat. Combine egg yolks, sugar, cornstarch, and salt. Mix with a little milk, then add to the milk in the pan and cook until it thickens. Add vanilla and butter. Cool sauce before filling the puffs.

To make the raspberry sauce, heat berries and put through a sieve to remove seeds. Place in a pan with sugar over medium heat. Add cornstarch mixed with a little water. Cook until it forms a syrup.

To assemble the dessert, fill each puff with custard sauce. Drizzle the raspberry sauce over each one before serving.

◆ *4 to 6 servings*

Lemon Curd Pie

Pastel de Limón ◆ *Argentina*

3 eggs

1 cup less 2 tablespoons sugar

⅓ cup of fresh lemon juice

6 tablespoons butter, cut into small
  pieces

1 tablespoon grated lemon zest

1 (9 inch) fully baked pie shell

3 egg whites

¼ cup sugar

Beat eggs and sugar in the top of a double boiler. Stir in fresh lemon juice
and add butter. Place the mixture over hot water and cook, stirring steadily,
until it is thickened and coats the spoon. Stir in grated lemon zest and let
the lemon filling cool. Pour the cooled filling into the pie shell. Preheat
oven to 400°F while you make the meringue.

Beat egg whites until peaks form. Then beat in sugar, a tablespoon at a
time, and continue to beat until the mixture is stiff but not dry. Fill a pastry
bag with meringue and cover the top of the lemon filling, making sure that
the meringue touches the crust all around. Bake in oven for 5 minutes or
until top is browned.

◆ *4 to 6 servings*

Almond Pudding

CREMA DE ALMENDRAS • *Peru*

Almond Custard Sauce

5 egg yolks
¼ cup sugar
2 cups milk

¼ teaspoon grated lemon zest
¼ teaspoon almond extract
½ cup slivered almonds

Meringue

1 envelope (1 tablespoon)
    unflavored gelatin
¼ cup cold water
5 egg whites
¾ cup sugar

½ teaspoon almond extract
¼ teaspoon grated lemon zest
Red food coloring
Green food coloring

To make the almond custard sauce, first separate the eggs, reserving whites to make the meringue. In the top of a double boiler, blend the egg yolks, sugar, milk, and lemon zest. Cook, stirring constantly, until the mixture thickens enough to coat the back of a wooden spoon. Remove from heat at once and set in a bowl of cold water to cool. Add almond extract and slivered almonds to the custard. Cover and chill.

To make the meringue, sprinkle gelatin into cold water. Let stand for 5 minutes to soften. Place over hot water until dissolved. Place the reserved egg whites in a large bowl. Add gelatin mixture to the egg whites. Beat whites with electric mixer at highest speed until they form a thick, white foam. Continue beating and add sugar, no more than 1 tablespoon at a time, sprinkling it gradually. When whites form soft, curving peaks, add almond extract and lemon zest and beat in thoroughly. Tint one third of the meringue pale pink with a few drops of red food coloring and tint another third of meringue with a few drops of green food coloring. Pile the pink, white, and green meringue mixtures side by side in a shallow bowl and cover with a cap of foil without it touching the meringue. Chill for at least 2 hours or as long as 5 hours.

To assemble the pudding, spoon meringue into dessert bowls and pour the almond custard sauce over each serving.

◆ *4 to 6 servings*

Chocolate Pudding

CREMA DE CHOCOLATE ◆ *Argentina*

This pudding may be served warm or chilled with ladyfingers.   —Lilly

3½ cups milk

1 cup unsweetened cocoa

3 tablespoons cornstarch

¼ teaspoon salt

1 cup sugar

1 egg, lightly beaten

1 egg yolk

2 ounces bittersweet chocolate,
    coarsely chopped

1 tablespoon vanilla extract

Combine 1 cup of the milk, cocoa, cornstarch, and salt in a large bowl. Stir well with a whisk. Set aside. Heat the remaining 2½ cups of milk in a large, heavy saucepan over medium heat until bubbles form around the edges (do not boil). Remove from heat. Stir in sugar with a whisk until sugar dissolves. Add cocoa mixture to the pan, stirring until blended. Bring to a boil over medium heat. Cook 2 minutes, stirring constantly. Combine egg and egg yolk in a bowl, stirring well. Gradually add milk mixture to egg mixture, stirring constantly. Return mixture to pan. Cook over medium heat until thick, about 2 minutes. Keep stirring. Remove from heat. Stir in chocolate and vanilla until the chocolate melts.

◆ *4 to 6 sevings*

Apple Bread Pudding

BUDIN DE PAN CON MANZANAS Y PASAS ◆ *Peru*

This pudding may be served with vanilla ice cream.   —Ana

8 thin slices of dried, firm bread

5 tablespoons butter

6 eggs

¼ cup sugar

¼ teaspoon cinnamon

½ cup golden raisins

1 cup heavy cream

1 cup apple juice

4 Golden Delicious apples, peeled,
    cored, and cut into rounds

3 tablespoons Calvados

Confectioners' sugar

Butter one side of the bread slices with 2 tablespoons of the butter. Lightly butter a 6-cup baking dish with 1 tablespoon butter. Lay the bread evenly in the dish. In a large bowl, whisk together eggs, sugar, cinnamon, and raisins until well blended. In a medium pan, combine cream and apple juice. Bring to a simmer over low heat. Gradually whisk the cream mixture into the egg mixture in a thin stream. Pour the custard over the bread and let stand, pushing the slices down, until the bread is saturated, about 20 minutes. Preheat the oven to 325°F. Place the baking dish in a roasting pan and add enough warm water to reach halfway up the sides of the dish. Bake in the center of the oven for 45 minutes or until the custard is set. In a large skillet, melt the remaining 2 tablespoons of butter. Add apples and sauté over high heat. Add the Calvados. Simmer until apples are tender. Preheat the broiler. Broil the bread pudding about 4 inches from the heat until the top is browned. Dust with confectioners' sugar. Mound the sautéed apples on top.

◆ *4 to 6 servings*

Lilly's Bread Pudding

Budin de Pan ◆ *Argentina*

Basic bread pudding is an uncomplicated partnership of bread and custard and a practical and tasty solution to the question of what to do with stale bread. The bread should be of good quality and at least several days old. I remember my mother making bread pudding once a week, gathering all the old pieces of bread from around her kitchen. Although it was a very plain pudding she would add some tasty raisins and a little port wine. I have made some adjustments to the original recipe. Serve this pudding warm with vanilla ice cream.   —Lilly

8 thin slices of dried, firm bread

5 tablespoons butter

6 eggs

¼ cup sugar

½ teaspoon cinnamon

2 cups half-and-half

4 Golden Delicious apples, peeled, cored, and quartered

2 teaspoons confectioners' sugar

Preheat the oven to 325°F. Butter one side of the bread slices with 2 tablespoons of the butter. Cut each slice into quarters. Lightly butter a baking dish with 1 tablespoon of the butter. Lay the bread evenly in the dish, overlapping the slices. In a large bowl, whisk together eggs, sugar, and cinnamon until well blended. In a medium saucepan, bring the half-and-half to a simmer over moderate heat. Gradually whisk half-and-half into egg mixture, in a thin stream. Pour the custard over the bread and let stand for 8 minutes. Push the slices down once or twice, until the bread is saturated. Place the baking dish in a roasting pan and add enough warm water to reach halfway up the side of the dish. Bake in the center of the oven for 45 to 50 minutes. Cut each apple quarter into 2 wedges. In a large skillet, melt the remaining 2 tablespoons of butter. Add apples and sauté over low heat until browned. Preheat the broiler. Broil the pudding about 4 inches from the heat until the top is browned. Dust with confectioners' sugar. Mound the sautéed apples on top. Sprinkle more sugar and a dash of cinnamon.

◆ *4 to 6 servings*

Nohemi's Custard

NATILLAS ◆ *Spain*

My sister, Raquel, who has a sweet tooth, always enjoyed the desserts Mamá made for us.   —Noemi

6 cups milk

6 tablespoons sugar

Zest of 1 lemon, grated

6 egg yolks

2 tablespoons cornstarch

Cinnamon

In a saucepan, heat milk, 4 tablespoons of the sugar, and lemon zest. Bring to a boil. In the meantime, beat the egg yolks, the remaining 2 tablespoons of sugar, and cornstarch in a large bowl. When the milk mixture is boiling, pour it over the egg mixture, little by little, stirring constantly. Pour mixture back into the saucepan and cook over medium heat, stirring constantly, without bringing the custard to a boil. There will be foam on top of the custard during cooking. Stir well until the foam disappears and the custard is smooth. Pour into a serving dish and refrigerate several hours. Sprinkle cinnamon on top before serving.

◆ *4 to 6 servings*

Rice Custard

Arroz con Leche ◆ *Peru*

Depending on my mood, I often add either ½ cup fresh pineapple cut in cubes, ½ cup shredded coconut, or ½ cup raisins to punch up the custard. —Ana

2 cups rice

1 can (14 ounces) sweetened
    condensed milk

1 can (12 ounces) evaporated milk

2 whole cloves

2 cinnamon sticks

Cinnamon

Cook rice in 3 cups salted water until tender, about 15 to 20 minutes. Add remaining ingredients and mix well. Simmer for 15 minutes. Sprinkle with cinnamon and serve warm.

◆ *4 to 6 servings*

Caramel Custard Cake

FLAN ◆ Spain

For many of the gatherings the *chicas* and I have together, I am asked to bring a *flan*. It has become one of the main desserts featured during our times together.   —Nohemi

1⅓ cups sugar	2 cups milk (not skim)
1 teaspoon hot water	2 teaspoons vanilla extract
3 tablespoons fresh lemon juice	1 egg
4 to 5 tablespoons water	5 egg yolks

In a metal mold pan, place ½ cup of the sugar, hot water, and lemon juice over medium heat until the color turns caramel. Swirl the mold until the walls of the mold are covered with caramel. Cool. Over medium heat, cook ½ cup of the sugar in a pan until the color turns caramel. Add the 4 to 5 tablespoons of water and stir until diluted. In a pan, boil milk and vanilla. Preheat oven to 350°F. In a big bowl, beat egg and egg yolks, adding the remaining ⅓ cup of the sugar. Beat well. Add the hot milk and the diluted caramel. Pour into the mold. Place the mold in a roasting pan. Add enough hot water to the pan to come halfway up the sides of the mold. Bake until custard is set, about 1 hour. Cool and run a knife around the mold to loosen the custard.

◆ *4 to 6 servings*

Caramel Custard Cake (Flan)

Poached Pears in Wine

PERAS AL VINO TINTO ◆ *Argentina*

Fruit, the focus of many desserts and some main courses as well, is very popular in Argentina. This is a wonderfully hearty dessert, well flavored by the wine. Add some good vanilla ice cream and this will be everyone's favorite indulgence.   —Lilly

6 Bartlett pears, peeled, leaving
   stems intact
1 cup water

½ cup sugar
1 cinnamon stick
1 bottle of red wine

Place the pears in acidulated water. In a saucepan bring water and sugar to a boil. Add the cinnamon stick. Immerse the pears in the syrup and cover them with wax paper. Cover, leaving the lid slightly ajar, and poach the pears over medium heat. After about 20 minutes, remove the lid and the wax paper and lift out a pear with a slotted spoon. Insert the tip of a knife into the base of the pear. When it meets light resistance, the pears are done. Pour the bottle of red wine into a heavy pot. Bring to a boil over high heat. Boil for 2 or 3 minutes to reduce slightly. Then add it to the pears and cook them gently for 5 minutes. Transfer pears to a bowl. Discard cinnamon stick. Pour half of the poaching liquid over the pears and let them cool. Cook the remaining poaching liquid over high heat until it has reduced to a thick syrup. Drain the pears and stand them upright in a large serving bowl. Ladle some of the wine syrup over the pears to glaze them and pour the rest into a bowl.

◆ *6 servings*

New Year's Bash

by Noemi

Every New Year's celebration at my mom's house included the eating of twelve grapes. Someone would clang out twelve bangs on a pot with a spoon in succession, and everyone would have to stuff a grape per clang in their mouths. You had to eat the grapes fast or the juice would run down your chin. It is a tradition that followed me after I left home and I introduced it to my friends during college. New Year's celebrations also included shrimp cocktail, cheese and crackers, and on at least one year a wonderful whiskey slush that Ana made when she held the feast at her house. Luckily, we kids were allowed to have a small cup of the slush.

Chocolate Mousse

Mousse de Chocolate ◆ *Peru*

S̲erve this mousse with sweetened whipped cream.   —Ana

2 ounces (2 squares) unsweetened
   chocolate

½ cup sugar

5 eggs, separated

1 cup finely ground roasted
   almonds

1 cup heavy cream

Break the chocolate into pieces and add to the top of a double boiler over boiling water. Add sugar and stir until chocolate is melted and the sugar is dissolved. Remove pan from the heat and beat in egg yolks, one at a time, beating well after each addition. Stir in almonds. Beat cream and fold it into the chocolate mixture. Beat egg whites until they stand in peaks and fold into the chocolate mixture. Mix well. Pour mixture into a soufflé dish and refrigerate for several hours.

◆ *4 to 6 servings*

Lemon Mousse

Mousse de Limón ◆ *Argentina*

2 envelopes (2 tablespoons)
  unflavored gelatin
¼ cup cold water
8 eggs, separated
1 cup sugar

½ cup strained fresh lemon juice
2 tablespoons grated lemon zest
24 ladyfingers
1 cup heavy cream
2 tablespoons confectioners' sugar

Sprinkle gelatin into cold water. Let stand for 5 minutes to soften. Beat egg yolks until they are slightly thickened and paler yellow. Add sugar gradually while beating constantly. Stir in lemon juice and 4 teaspoons of the grated lemon zest. Place over gently boiling water in the top of a double boiler, making sure water does not touch the bottom of the pot. Cook, stirring constantly, until the sauce forms a thick custard. Add softened gelatin to the hot mixture, stirring well, until the gelatin is dissolved. Pour the mixture into a bowl and let it cool, stirring occasionally. Line the sides and bottom of a 9-inch springform pan with the ladyfingers. Beat the egg whites until stiff and fold them into the cooked mixture. Pour mixture into the pan and refrigerate until the mousse sets firmly. To serve, remove the sides of the pan and using a large spatula, slide the mousse from the bottom onto a serving plate. Whip the cream with the confectioners' sugar and top the mousse with it and the remaining lemon zest.

◆ *4 to 6 servings*

Index

Spanish words are in *italics*.

aguacate (Spain and Colombia).
     See avocado
allspice, 138
Ana, 121–22
ananá (Argentina). *See*
     pineapple
apple cider, 136, 140, 141
apples
  fritters, 246
  Golden Delicious, 46, 257, 258
  green, 125, 136, 161
  in pastry, 244–45
  tart, 144
apricots, 125, 145, 162
arroz. See rice
artichokes, 92
asparagus, 8, 9
atún (tuna), 208
avocados, 7, 44, 48, 95

bacon, 22, 114
bananas, 37, 71, 72, 241, 242

bananas, in rum, 242
basil, 111, 113
beans, dried, 78
beef
  bouillon, 85, 96, 151, 166
  chuck, 161, 162
  filet mignon, 155, 164
  flank steak, 157, 158
  ground, 67, 69, 85, 97, 168
  kidneys, 158
  ribs, 160
  round, 161, 162
  round steaks, 166
  rump steak, 158
  short ribs, 158
  sirloin, 113, 151, 155, 158, 167
  stewing, 160
beef stew
  with dried fruit, 162
  Lilly's, 161
bistec. See beef
blood sausage, 158
bouillon, beef, 85, 96, 151, 166
bouillon, chicken, 31, 101

Bouquet garni, 29
brandy, 171
bread crumbs, 84, 104, 172, 216
  Italian, 168, 189, 191
brussel sprouts, 105
Butter, Maitre de Hotel, 164–65

cabbage, 26, 39, 46
cake
  almond and chocolate, 243
  banana and pineapple, 241
  caramel custard, 262
  Christmas, 227
calabacín. See zucchini
calamares. See squid
Calvados, 257
Canadian bacon, 22, 164, 191,
     212
canalones. See pasta
cantaloupe, 13
capers, 175
caramel custard, 262
carne. See beef
cashews, 216